PRELIMINARY

SUCCESS WITH BEC

THE NEW BUSINESS ENGLISH CERTIFICATES COURSE

WORKBOOK

HELEN STEPHENSON

NATIONAL GEOGRAPHIC LEARNING | CENGAGE Learning·

Australia • Brazil • Japan • Korea • Mexico • Singapore • Spain • United Kingdom • United States

Success with BEC Preliminary Workbook with Key
Helen Stephenson

Publisher: Nicholas Sheard

Head of Inventory: Jane Glendening

Manufacturing Team Lead: Paul Herbert

Production Controller: Tom Relf

Typesetter: Oxford Designers & Illustrators

Cover design: White Space

ISBN: 978-1-905992-03-4

National Geographic Learning
Cheriton House, North Way, Andover, Hampshire, SP10 5BE
United Kingdom

Cengage Learning is a leading provider of customized learning solutions with office locations around the globe, including Singapore, the United Kingdom, Australia, Mexico, Brazil and Japan. Locate your local office at: **international.cengage.com/region**

Cengage Learning products are represented in Canada by Nelson Education, Ltd.

Visit National Geographic Learning online at **ngl.cengage.com**

Visit our corporate website at **www.cengage.com**

Acknowledgements
The publishers would like to dedicate the Success with BEC series to the memory of its inspirational editor, David Riley.

Diagrams, copyright material and trademarks
A Welcome Invasion – Copyright Guardian News & Media Ltd 2007. Changes & Choices – Based on article Employees' Takeover of Loch Fyne – Oyster saves 100 jobs by Jeannette Oldham, reproduced with permission of The Scotsman. Problems & Solutions – Reproduced with the permission of Friends of the Earth. Summertown Publishing would also like to acknowledge the Business English Certificates Handbook (published by University of Cambridge ESOL Examinations) as the source of exam formats and rubrics in the Exam Spotlight lessons and other exam-type activities throughout the book.

Photography
Getty Images cover. Getty Images pages 5, 11. Henry Ford Motor. Company page 15. Ikea page 20. Getty images pages 28, 47, 53, 56, 61.

Illustrations
Pages 40 and 58 Illustrated by Phil Healey.

Printed in the United Kingdom by Ashford Colour Press Ltd.
Print Number: 09   Print Year: 2019

1.1 World of work

1 Read about three people's jobs (A–C) on a careers advice website and choose the correct job titles from the box.

> customer services manager
> human resources officer   lawyer
> marketing executive   office manager
> production manager   public relations officer
> retail manager   tourism officer   travel agent

Careers Advice

On this site you can find out what *real* people say about their jobs and what they *really* do day-to-day.

A _____

I love this job. I work long days, including Saturdays, and sometimes Sunday mornings too, but I enjoy it. I'm responsible for the success of the shop – meeting our sales targets, basically – but I always try to exceed our targets and I <u>organise</u> special promotions. We often get a bonus from head office. On a typical day, I get here early in the morning and I check the deliveries. I'm very strict about quality control. I help the staff organise the displays and then I open the shop. I manage a staff of ten. I organise their shifts and process their salaries. My assistant manager supervises their day-to-day work. For me, the only difficult aspect of this job is the accounts – I'm terrible at maths.

B _____

I work a typical working week, Monday to Friday, which is great. I never come to work on a Saturday or Sunday. I'm responsible for managing all the administration in our office. I'm usually at my computer most of the day. I check and process the office accounts and I supervise the security and administrative staff. There's a lot of paperwork: I deal with all the payments related to the staff and the office. In this job, you need to pay attention to detail and I enjoy that aspect. The staff here sometimes think that I'm very strict – about personal phone calls and so on – but it's my job to reduce our office costs. I don't like wasting the company's money.

C _____

In my job, I usually work every day of the week, including holidays. I sometimes get a day off in the middle of the week. I don't mind because I get long holidays in the winter. My job is quite interesting because of all the people I meet. I talk to people of different nationalities every day, especially in the summer holiday season. I answer people's queries and give information about the area. Another part of my job that I enjoy is setting up exhibitions to promote the area. I sometimes lead tours to local attractions – that can be great fun. To the visitor, we represent this town and perhaps this country – that's why I like to do my job well.

2 Match each person to a text, A, B or C. Which person:

0 is responsible for meeting sales targets?   A

1 doesn't work at weekends?   _____

2 meets people from many countries?   _____

3 deals with different enquiries?   _____

4 uses a computer a lot?   _____

5 often starts work early?   _____

3 Underline the verbs for job functions in each text. Write them below in the infinitive form.

Text A

0 *organise* special promotions

1 c_____ deliveries

2 h_____ staff

3 m_____ staff

4 p_____ salaries

5 s_____ day-to-day work

Text B

6 c_____ accounts

7 p_____ accounts

8 s_____ staff

9 d_____ w_____ payments

10 r_____ office costs

Text C

11 a_____ queries

12 g_____ information

13 s_____ u_____ exhibitions

14 l_____ tours

15 r_____ the town / country

The present simple

4 Complete the text with the present simple form of the verbs in brackets.

I (**0**) _work_ (work) in the head office of a foreign currency exchange agency. The company (**1**) _____ (have) offices all over the world, in airports and in city centres. My job (**2**) _____ (be) a bit boring at times, especially the routine tasks. On the other hand, it's a responsible position – we all (**3**) _____ (deal with) large sums of money every day. A lot of our work (**4**) _____ (be) automatic: a machine (**5**) _____ (count) the money, for example. I prefer that, because I (**6**) _____ (not like) to make mistakes. We (**7**) _____ (not often have) problems with false money: I think everybody (**8**) _____ (know) that our machines (**9**) _____ (be) very sophisticated. However, people occasionally (**10**) _____ (try) to use false credit cards to buy foreign currency.

Adverbs and expressions of frequency

5 Rewrite each sentence with the time expressions in the correct positions.

0 Do you drive to work? *usually*

Do you usually drive to work?

1 He doesn't work late. *usually*

_____

2 I work at weekends. *never*

_____

3 He visits clients. *twice a month*

_____

4 I am at my desk by 8am. *normally*

_____

5 Do they give press conferences? *every week*

_____

6 She isn't behind schedule. *often*

_____

7 We finish work early. *often / on Fridays*

_____

8 Our department organises training sessions.
sometimes / at weekends

_____

9 He is late for work. *occasionally / on Mondays*

_____

6 Look at the chart, which shows the results of a survey into employee honesty, and complete the sentences.

1 In Company X, employees never _____ .

2 In Company _____ , staff sometimes make personal phone calls at work.

3 In Company Y, staff rarely _____ .

4 In Company _____ , employees rarely arrive late or leave early.

5 In Company _____ , staff often surf the Internet.

7 Now write three sentences about each company for activities F–H.

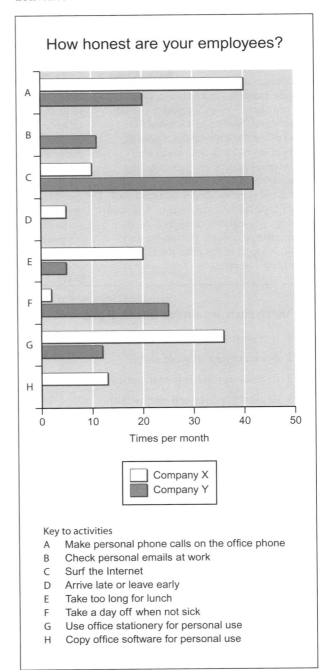

How honest are your employees?

Times per month

Company X
Company Y

Key to activities
A   Make personal phone calls on the office phone
B   Check personal emails at work
C   Surf the Internet
D   Arrive late or leave early
E   Take too long for lunch
F   Take a day off when not sick
G   Use office stationery for personal use
H   Copy office software for personal use

1.2 Personal and professional details

Pronunciation

1 Write the remaining letters of the alphabet in the correct column, according to their sounds. Check your answers to exercise 1 in the answer key before you do exercise 2.

day	*see*	*pen*	*eye*	*go*	*you*	*car*
A	B	F	I	O	Q	R
___	___	___	___		___	
___	___				___	
___	___	___				
	___	___				
	___	___				
	___	___				
	___					

2 Now practise saying the alphabet. Read each column in exercise 1 vertically.

3 Verbs ending in *-s* are pronounced in one of three ways:

/z/ **as in** *goes*	/s/ **as in** *works*	/iz/ **as in** *finishes*
_____	_____	_____
_____	_____	_____
_____	_____	_____
_____	_____	_____

Write the following verbs in the correct columns above.

tries	organises	gets	checks
helps	opens	manages	processes
enjoys	visits	gives	arranges

At the annual meeting

4 Put the words in the correct order to make greetings.

1 again nice hi see Anya to you

_____

2 I'm hello Ross McGovern

_____

3 me you excuse are Bart Roland ?

_____

4 you how hello Ms Wiseman are ?

_____

5 Delemus me name is your excuse ?

_____

6 good my name's Maya Lund morning

_____

5 Match the greetings 1–6 in exercise 4 with the responses A–F below.

☐ A Yes, I am.
☐ B I'm fine, thanks.
☐ C Hi, pleased to meet you, Ross. I'm Brian.
☐ D How do you do?
☐ E No, I'm afraid it isn't.
☐ F It's nice to see you, too.

Personal and professional profiles

6 Write questions for these answers using the prompts in the box.

> What / do?   Who / work for?
> How often / show your collection?
> ~~What time / start work?~~   Where / from?
> Do / like your job?   Who / buy / your designs?
> Where / be / your studio?   Be / ambitious?
> Why / be / in Paris?

0 What time do you start work?

I start work at 8am.

1 _____

I'm a fashion designer.

2 _____

I work for YSL.

3 _____

Yes, I love my job.

4 _____

My studio is in the centre of Paris.

5 _____

Because it's the fashion centre of the world.

6 _____

I show my collection twice a year, in spring and in autumn.

7 _____

Yes, I'm very ambitious. I want to have my own fashion label.

8 _____

I'm from Birmingham, in England.

9 _____

Lots of celebrities and film stars buy my clothes.

7 Use the information in exercise 6 to write a profile of the fashion designer, Raffi. Change the pronouns and verb forms, as appropriate.

Raffi is from Birmingham, in England. He ...

_____

_____

_____

_____

_____

_____

_____

Exam writing skills: proof reading

8 Read the text and find six errors in spelling, punctuation and grammar.

> Our global **PLA** community   **PLA** Inc.
>
> my profile ——————————————
>
> **Katherine Pereira**   *This page has received 374 visits*
> K_perreira@pla.com   *Click here to update profile*
>
> *Hi everyone,*
>
> *I'm Katherine, but my friend's call me Kate. My name is english, but I'm from Lisbon. I'm lawyer and I work in the head ofice of the Legal Department at PLA. I specialise in insurance contracts. In my spare time, I like marathon runing and fotography. You can see my pictures if you click here. I hope you like them!*

9 Read the profile you wrote in exercise 7 and check your spelling, punctuation and grammar.

1.3 Reading Test: Part One

In Part One of the Reading Test there are four short texts. Each text is followed by one multiple choice question. For each question, make sure you can say why the two incorrect options are wrong.

1 Which option is correct, A, B or C?

1

PEEJAY ELECTRICS

Deliveries accepted Mondays and Thursdays ONLY.

    A The shop accepts deliveries in the mornings only.
    B The shop takes deliveries twice a week.
    C The shop delivers goods two days a week.

---

2 Say why the other two options are incorrect.

3 Repeat exercises 1 and 2 for texts 2–4 below.

2

Be Positive! Training Conference

Please sign in at reception, collect your welcome pack and have your photo taken for your conference ID badge.

Conference participants should
    A present identity documents at reception.
    B check out when they leave.
    C go to reception when they arrive.

3

Computer back-up and system maintenance every Friday 16.30–17.30.

The IT department does routine work
    A on Friday afternoons.
    B on Friday mornings.
    C at half past six on a Friday.

4

Spar Minimarket
We are closed for holidays from 2/2 until 12/2 inclusive.

The shop
    A is open in February.
    B is closed on the first of February.
    C is open at the end of February

2.1 Work in progress

The present continuous

1 Read the extract from a company newsletter and complete the text with the present continuous form of the verbs in brackets.

New IT systems for all staff

Major improvements in IT are coming to all offices

IT gives us essential tools to do our jobs, and the IT Improvement Project (**0**) is delivering (deliver) those tools. The aim of the project is to increase efficiency in all aspects of our business through better in-company IT systems. The project's first big success is the new email application: after a very successful trial at head office, we (**1**) _____ (extend) our in-house email system across the whole company. The project manager, Fraser King, says, 'We (**2**) _____ (look) at things that really make a difference and we (**3**) _____ (improve) them. My team (**4**) _____ (hold) meetings in all the divisions, and they (**5**) _____ (use) face-to-face interviews and online surveys to collect information from users. Our key question is "What (**6**) _____ (not / work) well for you and why not?"' Fraser is in the middle of a four-week fact-finding trip – he (**7**) _____ (visit) Sydney, Bangkok and Seattle this month, where he (**8**) _____ (coordinate) the project with local managers. 'I (**9**) _____ (give) lots of presentations about the project – I want everyone to understand what we (**10**) _____ (do). So far the response is very positive and people are enthusiastic. Everyone's looking forward to using better, more efficient IT tools.'

2 Look at Fraser King's schedule for his visit to Sydney. Write a sentence for each activity using the verbs in the box.

> discuss   interview   give   visit
> ~~have~~   leave   meet

0 On Day 1, he's having a breakfast meeting with the IT manager, Australia.

Day 1 (Thurs 10th)
am   breakfast meeting – IT manager, Australia
       department heads – meetings until lunchtime
pm   presentation of project to local staff

Day 2 (Fri 11th)
am   with IT manager – tour of Sydney offices and factories
       interviews with local staff
pm   with IT manager – project schedules

Day 3 (Sat 12th)
Free

Day 4 (Sun 13th)
Night flight to Bangkok

---

3 Match sentences 1–6 with responses A–F. Then say whether each exchange refers to (1) an action that is happening now, (2) a temporary activity or (3) a fixed arrangement in the future.

1 What are you working on at the moment?	A He's having lunch, I think.	
2 Where's Sam?	B Really? Where?	
3 We're using the small meeting room this week.	C No, sorry. I'm leaving for Brussels at two o'clock.	
4 Why is the printer making that noise?	D The new Christmas promotion.	2
5 Can we talk about the IT project this afternoon?	E I don't know. Perhaps there's some paper stuck in it.	
6 We're opening four new shops next month.	F I know, they're painting the main room.	

Temporary jobs

4 Read the lists of job responsibilities for a project manager and a team leader. Complete the lists using the verbs in the box.

> complete ~~employ~~ give hire
> hold meet set supervise

Project manager

0 *employ* project staff

1 _____ targets for each phase of the project

2 _____ meetings with management

3 _____ project on schedule

Team leader

4 _____ the work of the team

5 _____ weekly updates to project manager

6 _____ deadlines agreed with project manager

7 _____ temporary staff if necessary

5 Read the email about a summer job in an investment bank and decide whether sentences 1–5 are 'Right' or 'Wrong'. If there is not enough information to answer 'Right' or 'Wrong', choose 'Doesn't say'.

1 Camille has a temporary job at Merrill Lynch.
   A Right　　B Wrong　　C Doesn't say

2 Camille is working in the front office for the summer.
   A Right　　B Wrong　　C Doesn't say

3 Fatima is applying for a permanent job at the bank.
   A Right　　B Wrong　　C Doesn't say

4 Mulligan only employs university graduates.
   A Right　　B Wrong　　C Doesn't say

5 Camille is going back to university after the summer.
   A Right　　B Wrong　　C Doesn't say

6 Look at the underlined words in the text and find synonyms for these words.

1 choice　　　　_____

2 customers　　_____

3 excellent　　　_____

4 share dealers　_____

5 temporary　　_____

6 university course _____

Hi Fatima,

How's it going? Are you enjoying the summer? How's your summer job at Merrill Lynch going? I'm having a <u>great</u> time here at Mulligan! The people are really friendly and I'm learning so much. I'm getting lots of experience – it's quite different to everything we're doing at university, isn't it? I'm working in 'Operations', where they deal with all the transactions between the bank's <u>clients</u> and the <u>traders</u>. Next week I'm spending three days with the traders in the front office – that should be exciting! Which department are you working in at Merrill Lynch? Are they paying you lots of money? Are you thinking about applying for a permanent job there next year? Here at Mulligan they have a training scheme for university graduates – it sounds like a really good <u>option</u>. They give you a <u>short-term</u> contract, for six months, while they're training you, and the money is great. You can try out different jobs and find out what you like and what you are good at. Anyway, that's all for next year – first, I have to finish my <u>degree</u>!

By the way, any news from Harry? I think he's still trekking in Nepal, but I don't think he's getting my emails. And Lucinda says she hates her sailing trip and she can't wait to come home!

Anyway, let me know how you're getting on. Look forward to hearing from you soon.

Love,

Camille

2.2 Making arrangements

Arranging a meeting

1 Match Roger's responses (A–E) to the gaps (1–5) to complete the conversation.

Fraser Hello, Roger. It's Fraser. Can we meet this morning to discuss the project schedule?

Roger (1) _____

Fraser OK, how about this afternoon?

Roger (2) _____

Fraser Well, I'm meeting the managing director at half past four, so before then.

Roger (3) _____

Fraser That doesn't give us much time.

Roger (4) _____

Fraser Yes, that's fine.

Roger (5) _____

Fraser Great. Thanks, Roger.

A How does half past three sound?

B OK. See you then.

C What about three o'clock, in that case?

D Yes, that sounds fine. What time are you free?

E Hi, Fraser. Sorry, I can't. I'm busy all morning.

Pronunciation

2 Say these times and dates aloud and decide which parts are stressed. Then complete the rules below by choosing the correct option in bold.

09.15	12.30	2.20	6.19
1990	1314	2015	1680

1 The numbers 20, 30, 40, 50, 60, 70, 80 and 90 are stressed on the **first/second** syllable.

2 The numbers 13, 14, 15, 16, 17, 18 and 19 are stressed on the **first/second** syllable.

3 Practise saying the numbers 20 to 90 and 13 to 19 aloud.

4 Write out these times and dates in words and mark the stresses. Practise saying each one aloud.

15.30	fif<u>teen</u> <u>thir</u>ty
13.40	_____
19.20	_____
18.50	_____
20.15	_____
Feb 17th	<u>Feb</u>ruary the seven<u>teen</u>th
Dec 19th	_____
Oct 15th	_____
Nov 30th	_____
Aug 20th	_____

Prepositions of time: *at, in, on*

5 Complete the sentences by choosing the correct prepositions.

1 Our employees get a bonus *at / in* Christmas.

2 The seminar is *on / in* Tuesday.

3 We're moving offices *on / in* June.

4 They're launching the new model *in / on* 2009.

5 He's making a press announcement *on / at* six o'clock.

6 They're opening the shop *at / in* weekends now.

7 I switch off my mobile phone *on / in* the evening.

8 We hold a progress meeting *at / on* the last day of the month.

9 She works from home *at / on* Mondays and Tuesdays.

10 Our sales usually drop *on / in* the winter.

Invitations

6 Read the headers of two emails, an invitation (A) and a reply (B). Then read the lines from the two emails and decide which email they belong to. Put the lines in the correct order and copy out each email under the correct header.

Email A: an invitation

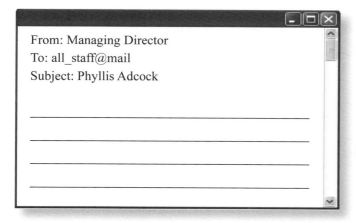

From: Managing Director
To: all_staff@mail
Subject: Phyllis Adcock

_____

_____

_____

_____

Email B: a reply

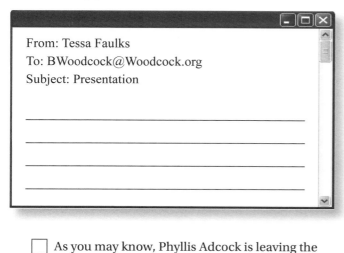

From: Tessa Faulks
To: BWoodcock@Woodcock.org
Subject: Presentation

_____

_____

_____

_____

☐ As you may know, Phyllis Adcock is leaving the company at the end of the week.

☐ Many thanks for the invitation to your presentation on Tuesday 12th.

☐ I invite you all to join Phyllis, myself and the rest of the management team

☐ I'm afraid I'm visiting our Italian subsidiary next week and

☐ on Friday lunchtime, for an informal leaving party.

☐ so I won't be able to attend.

☐ Drinks and snacks will be served in the board room from 1pm.

☐ Please be prompt.

☐ Good luck with the presentation!

7 Read Email A and underline the information about *what, what time / when* and *where*. What other important information is given?

8 Write B Woodcock's original invitation to Tessa Faulks. Use Email A as a guide. Make sure you include information about *what, when* and *where*.

9 Write a note to Phyllis Adcock. Explain that you can't attend her leaving party, give a reason and apologise. Wish her luck in her future career. Use Email B as a guide.

Exam writing skills: following task instructions

10 Read the notes about a seminar, then read the invitation. Find and correct three mistakes in the invitation.

Seminar invitations
- `future trends in IT'
- science museum
- 17/07
- starts 10am
- for all IT professionals, especially systems managers
- registration closes 10/07

From: A_Parlett@systools.co.uk
To: BWoodcock@Woodcock.org
Subject: IT seminar

I am writing to invite you to our annual seminar on Future Trends in IT. This year the seminar is taking place at the Science Museum, in July. It is from 9am to 1pm. It is open to all IT professionals, and it is of particular interest to IT systems managers. Please confirm your attendance. Registration closes in June.

We look forward to seeing you at the seminar again this year.

Best regards

Andrew Parlett

The Writing Test comes immediately after the Reading Test. You have 1 hour and 30 minutes to do the Reading and Writing Tests.

The Writing Test has two parts:

In Part One, you have to write a piece of internal communication, ie to someone in the company. You have to write 30–40 words.

In Part Two, you have to write a piece of business correspondence, ie to someone outside the company. You have to write 60–80 words.

1 Read the information about the Writing Test. Write Part One or Part Two next to the texts below.

A _____

Hi Fiona,

The IT manager is coming this afternoon, around 3pm, but I'm leaving early to catch the flight to London. Can you meet him on my behalf? All the notes for the meeting are on my desk.

Thanks a lot,

Charlie

B _____

Dear Bill,

This is to confirm the points we agreed on at our meeting yesterday, 13 March.

As the main contractor, you are responsible for hiring all the construction workers and for supervising the day-to-day progress of the project. The additional cost of employing extra workers, if necessary, comes from your budget. Phase 1 is currently running two weeks behind schedule; you will give daily updates to me, the project manager, for the rest of phase 1.

Regards,

Gavin Lowe

2 Which exam questions 1–3 matches text A?

1

- You are unable to go to a meeting because you have to fly to London.
- Write a **note** to your colleague:
  - asking him / her to represent you at the meeting
  - explaining when and where the meeting is
  - telling him / her to call you if you need any more information.

2

- You are arranging a meeting between the IT manager and your department.
- Write a **memo** to your staff:
  - explaining the reason for the meeting
  - giving the time and date of the meeting
  - asking everybody to attend punctually.

3

- You are unable to meet a scheduled visitor because you have to fly to London.
- Write a **note** to your colleague:
  - saying who is coming to the office
  - explaining why you can't meet him / her
  - asking your colleague to have the meeting with the visitor, using the information on your desk.

3 Write the texts to answer exam questions 1 and 2.

_____

_____

_____

_____

_____

3.1 Company biography

The past simple

1 Read about events in the business world over the last 100 years and complete the sentences with the past simple form of the verbs in the box. Check the verbs in your dictionary if necessary.

> begin   buy   crash   ~~develop~~   end   force
> form   launch   invent   merge   sign

Business events – the last 100 years

1912   Henry Ford (**0**) *developed* the idea of the production line to mass produce cars.

1929   The Wall Street stock market (**1**) _____ and ended the consumer boom of the 1920s.

1933   The 3M company (**2**) _____ Scotch tape, the first self-adhesive tape.

1946   Masaru Ibuka and Akio Morita (**3**) _____ Tokyo Tsushin Kogyo K.K. (later known as Sony), making tape recorders.

1957   Six European countries (**4**) _____ the Treaty of Rome and founded the European Economic Community, to promote free trade in Europe.

1967   Telefunken made the first colour televisions, and colour broadcasts (**5**) _____ in Europe.

1973   The first oil crisis (**6**) _____ companies around the world to increase their prices. As a result, both inflation and unemployment increased dramatically.

1985   In April, Coca-Cola (**7**) _____ 'New Coke'. It was a marketing failure and they reintroduced 'Classic Coke' two months later.

1995   The 'dot-com boom' of Internet companies began, creating 'dot-com millionaires'. The boom (**8**) _____ in 2000.

1999   Two oil companies, Exxon and Mobil, (**9**) _____, becoming the world's largest company.

2005   The Chinese company Lenovo (**10**) _____ IBM's PC division.

2 Write questions in the past simple about some of the information in the text using the prompts below.

1 What / Henry Ford / produce?

_____

2 When / be / the Wall Street Crash?

_____

3 What / be / the aim of the EEC?

_____

4 Where / colour TV broadcasts / begin?

_____

5 Be / 'New Coke' a success?

_____

6 How long / the dot-com boom / last?

_____

3 Write the answers to questions 1–6 in exercise 2.

1 _____

2 _____

3 _____

4 _____

5 _____

6 _____

Company profiles

4 Read the title and subtitle of the business magazine article. Write down three companies you expect to read about.

5 Read the article quickly and underline the companies it talks about. Do they include the companies you wrote down?

6 Read the text again and choose the best answer (A, B or C) for each question.

1 IBM sold its first products
   A all over the world.
   B in Canada and the USA.
   C to British scientists.

2 Vodafone began operating in
   A the UK.
   B the 1990s.
   C 30 countries.

3 Vodafone grew when it
   A merged with another UK network.
   B introduced digital technology.
   C bought other telephone businesses.

4 Mr Proctor and Mr Gamble
   A were originally business partners in Ireland.
   B met in the USA and became business partners.
   C came to the USA together to start a business.

5 In the 20th century, P&G
   A expanded their candle business.
   B sold the same line of goods.
   C launched new products on the market.

7 Read the text again and find verbs that mean the same as these.

Paragraph 1
finished   _____
produced   _____
sold   _____

Paragraph 2
grew   _____
bought   _____
introduced   _____

Paragraph 3
convinced   _____
designed and made _____

Business Giants

A look at some of the world's key companies: old, new and very powerful

In the 20th century, businesses and industry changed in many ways. The 'industrial age' ended and the 'information age' began. But one famous information age company, IBM, actually started operations in the 19th century, in 1889. Now an IT giant, IBM employs over 350,000 people around the world and has a revenue of about $100 billion. In its early days, the company made business machines for time-keeping and data-processing, and it marketed its products in the USA and Canada. IBM didn't develop the first totally electronic and digital computer but they designed and produced the first digital computers for commercial purposes.

Digital technology was essential to the success of companies such as Vodafone, the biggest telecommunications network company in the world. Vodafone provides mobile phone services to over 200 million customers in nearly 30 countries. In 1984, the company started operating one of only two UK mobile phone networks. In the 1990s, the company expanded; it acquired other communications companies around the world and launched new services. Currently, Vodafone's revenue is around £30,000m.

In 1837, a partnership between two brothers-in-law made candles and soap. 170 years later, the company, now a global corporation, owns brands such as Pringles, Braun, Duracell, Gillette and Pampers. William Proctor and James Gamble arrived in the USA from England and Ireland respectively. They met through marrying sisters, Olivia and Elizabeth Norris, whose father persuaded his sons-in-law to go into business together. The company survived the introduction of domestic electric lighting (this was the end of the market for candles) and the economic depression of the 1930s. They invested money in research and developed many new products in the first half of the 20th century. In the second half, P&G expanded by buying other companies. With over 135,000 employees today, P&G has a revenue of about $75,000m.

Company activities

1 Complete the sentences by choosing the correct verbs.

1 Coca-Cola *sold / provided* Coke in cans for the first time in 1955.

2 In the 1930s, Hollywood studios *manufactured / produced* over 50 classic films.

3 IBM *managed / designed* some of the first personal computers.

4 In the 1990s, The Body Shop *imported / distributed* many of its raw materials from India.

5 Bayer first *organised / marketed* acetosal as Aspirin in 1899.

6 The News Corporation *published / supplied* over 80 newspapers and magazines last year.

Pronunciation

2 Verbs ending in *-ed* are pronounced in one of three ways:

/d/ **as in** *planned*	/t/ **as in** *produced*	/id/ **as in** *started*
_____	_____	_____
_____	_____	_____
_____	_____	_____
_____	_____	_____
_____	_____	_____

Write the following verbs in the correct columns above.

crashed designed developed distributed expanded forced imported launched manufactured marketed merged organised provided published supplied

3 Read the notes for a presentation about ExxonMobil. Practise giving the presentation and record yourself.

ExxonMobil Corporation

Type of company	Public
Began operations	1999 Exxon and Mobil merged
Original name	(1882) Standard Oil
Headquarters	Texas, USA
Chairman/CEO	Rex W. Tillerson
Products	Fuels, Lubricants, Petrochemicals
Revenue (2006)	$377.635 billion USD
Employees	around 100,000

Exam writing skills: proof reading

4 Read the news item and find six errors in spelling, punctuation and grammar.

Business is begining to recover from the stock market mini-crash last wednesday. The index rise by three points yesterday and there was an increase in activity in all sectors. Experts says that the fall in share prices last week was not a real crash, but part of a normal cicle and not unusual in october.

Production, sales and share prices

5 Look at the graph of the share price of a dot-com company, theGlobe.com. Then put sentences A–M in the correct order.

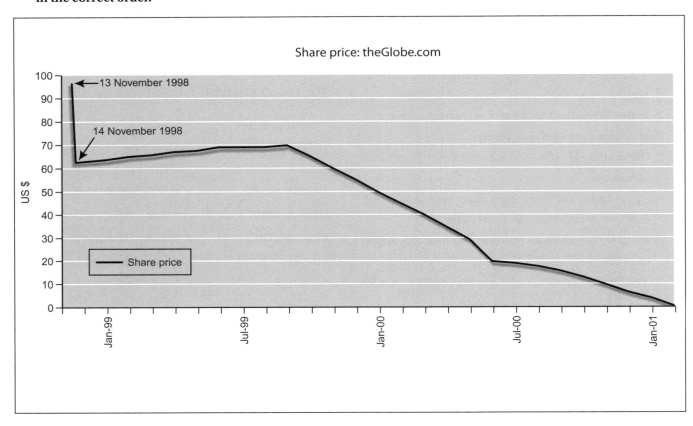

Share price: theGlobe.com

Paragraph 1

A In the first month, the site _____ (have) over 44,000 visits.

B It _____ (be) an Internet chat site.

C Two students, Stephan Paternot and Todd Krizelman, _____ (found) theGlobe.com in 1994.

Correct order ☐ ☐ ☐

Paragraph 2

D But the share price _____ (rise) to $97 before it then _____ (drop) to $63.50.

E On the first day of trading on the stock exchange, the share price _____ (be) set at $9.

F That day, the company _____ (set) a stock market record with an increase of 606% over the initial share price.

G The company _____ (sell) 3.1 million shares and _____ (raise) $27.9 million.

H The site _____ (grow) and, in 1998, theGlobe.com _____ (become) a public company.

I Paternot and Krizelman now _____ (have) personal fortunes of about $100 million each.

Correct order ☐ ☐ ☐ ☐ ☐ ☐

Paragraph 3

J In 1999 the dot-com boom _____ (start) to end.

K In 2001, Paternot and Krizelman _____ (lose) control of the company.

L Eventually, it _____ (drop) to less than ten cents.

M TheGlobe.com's share price _____ (fall) rapidly.

Correct order ☐ ☐ ☐ ☐

6 Complete sentences A–M with the past simple form of the verbs in brackets.

3.3 Listening Test: Part One

In Part One of the Listening Test there are eight short conversations or monologues. Each one is accompanied by one multiple choice question which can be text or pictures. Predicting what you are going to hear is a key skill for this part of the test.

1 For questions 1–4, write as many words as you can think of connected to the topics.

2 Look at boxes A–D on the right and match them to questions 1–4. Then tick (✓) the words in each box which are connected to the topics.

1 Which package was most successful?

2 Which transport do they choose?

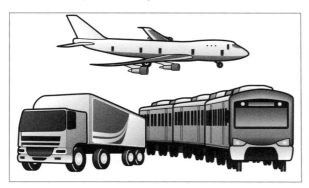

3 Which graph is correct?

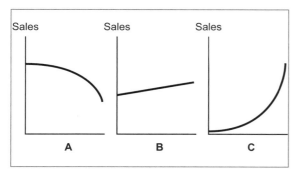

4 What event is the company announcing?
  A record profits
  B a new product
  C a new CEO

A

drop
fall
increase
invent
months
office
rise
safe
sold
trend

B

application
bottle
carton
can
customers
drink
fly
packet
sales
time

C

air
computer
lorry
paper
plane
rail
road
share
train
truck

D

CV
experience
launch
leader
market
material
memo
millions
performance
system

4.1 International business

EU import ban

1 Match the words 1–6 to the definitions A–F to complete the sentences.

1 A carrier	A buys the imported goods in large quantities.
2 A consumer	B transports the goods by air, sea, road or rail.
3 A freight forwarder	C arranges the transport of the goods from country A to country B.
4 A manufacturer	D buys the imported goods to sell to individuals.
5 A retailer	E produces goods in country A.
6 A wholesaler	F buys goods for personal use in country B.

2 Write the words 1–6 in the correct order to show the supply chain.

manufacturer → _____ → _____ →
_____ → _____ → _____

3 Read the book review and choose the best title.

A A Scandinavian success story

B Shopping in Scandinavia

C How to export goods to Scandinavia

4 Read the article again and complete the sentences.

1 There are 20 million _____ in Scandinavia.

2 Scandinavia produces 3% of the world's
_____ .

3 Many _____ are manufactured in one country and sold in another.

4 Lego, Volvo and Ikea are all Scandinavian
_____ .

5 Scandinavian companies are _____ abroad because they take risks.

5 Complete the table with the missing nouns.

verb	noun – thing	noun – person
compete	_____	competitor
consume	consumption	_____
export	_____	_____
import	_____	_____
produce	_____	_____
retail	_____	_____
sell	_____	_____
ship	shipment	_____
supply	supplies	_____
transport	transport	_____

The Scandinavian countries have a relatively small population of about 20 million. That's about 0.3% of the world's population, but the Scandinavians produce 3% of the world's exports.

A new book* looks at this export success and at the reasons behind it. One of the interesting things about Scandinavian exports is that they export brands as well as goods. Many countries manufacture goods that they then ship around the world to different retailers. The clothing industry is a good example. The customer doesn't know where the shirt or dress was made unless they look at the label inside. But customers all over the world who shop at Ikea know that they are buying Swedish goods. The same is true for the Scandinavian brands Lego, Absolute, Volvo, H&M, Saab and AstraZeneca. These companies discovered they could sell their brand as well as their product. Ikea, for example, decorated their new UK shops with Swedish

books. 'I don't think a British retailer could do that in France or Spain,' says one retail analyst.

According to the book, Scandinavian companies succeed abroad because they can accept the idea of taking risks. With such a small domestic market, expansion abroad is essential, and risk is part of that.

*The Viking Manifesto, by Steve Strid and Claes Andreasson. Published by Cyan.

Modal verbs: *can/could* and *should*

6 Complete the sentences with *can, can't, could* or *couldn't.*

1 _____ you speak Japanese? There's a Japanese man at reception.

2 Sorry for the delay in returning your call – I _____ find your phone number.

3 We _____ arrange transport by sea or air to all major ports.

4 I didn't use Speedy Shippers last time because they _____ guarantee next-day delivery.

5 They _____ supply 20,000 units, but they _____ deliver until next week.

6 The shipment is in the port, so it _____ be available today or tomorrow.

7 This is urgent. I need the report today. I _____ wait until tomorrow.

8 We're making good progress on the new shop. It _____ be ready by next week.

7 Decide which option is <u>not</u> possible in each sentence.

1 Fiona, *can / could / should* you give me a price for this shipment, please?

2 You *can't / should / could* use ZP Express; they're fast and efficient.

3 *Should / Can / Could* I borrow your mobile for a moment?

4 I'm afraid you *can / can't / shouldn't* use the office phone for personal calls.

5 *Can / Could / Couldn't* you help me?

6 You *shouldn't / couldn't / can't* leave work early every day.

7 *Should / Could / Can* you take this phone call for me please? I'm late for a meeting.

8 It *can't / shouldn't / should* take three months to repair a photocopier! That's ridiculous!

8 Read the advertisement, which shows services offered by a shipping company. Decide which of the sentences 1–5 are true.

1 The company can't arrange transport for private individuals.

2 Individual clients should phone the company for information.

3 The company can help with customs procedures.

4 The company can't ship goods by air.

5 The company can deliver to Europe in two days.

COULSON FREIGHT
International Shipping Company
London, UK

Logistics and freight forwarding for large and small companies and individuals*

Our services include:

Road – import & export

Air freight services

Sea freight – container import & export

Customs clearance

House removals (inside Europe only)

Express service to European destinations in 48 hours

Frequent services to all countries
Information: ... +44 181 83787487

Contact us for full details

Dealing with complaints

1 Read the letter of complaint to Westco Transport and put the sections in the correct order.

1 ☐

2 ☐

3 ☐

4 ☐

5 ☐

6 ☐

7 ☐

A J Hallcro

B Could you please send us the correct invoice and inform us about the claims procedure for the damaged monitors?

C Dear Sir or Madam,

D I am writing about your invoice 982/08 for the transport of our office furniture to new premises on 3rd March.

E In addition, four PC monitors were damaged during transportation. Our contract with you states that you will pay compensation for damaged goods.

F The original quotation for this work was €1,500. However, the invoice you sent us is for €2,750, and contains several errors. For example, the move took only one day, not two days as detailed in your invoice.

G Yours sincerely

---

2 Read the letter again and complete the notes made by the administrator at Westco.

From: (1) _____
Complaint about: (2) _____
                 damage to (3) _____
Action: check invoice 982/08
                 Write to Mr Hallcro about
                 (4) _____

3 Read the notes made by another customer of Westco. Write a letter of complaint to Westco. Use the letter in exercise 1 as a model.

- Give your reason for writing in paragraph 1.
- Give details of the problem in paragraph 2.
- Say what action you want Westco to take in paragraph 3.

Westco invoice 982/09 – moving office furniture – 4th & 5th March

original quotation €2,750 – invoice €1,500 – is this a mistake? Charged for only one day?

Get them to check and send new invoice.

Dear Sir or Madam,

_____
_____
_____
_____
_____
_____
_____
_____
_____
_____
_____
_____

Exam writing skills: proof reading

4 Read the letter you wrote in exercise 3 and check that you have included all the information in the task instructions. Check that the information is correct.

will

5 Decide what you could say in each situation. Write sentences using *will* and the words in brackets.

0 Your colleague has to take a package to reception but is very busy. (take)
Don't worry, I'll take it.

1 Your boss wants a copy of a report urgently. (photocopy / now)
_____
_____

2 You're working late a lot. Your family is complaining. (finish early / tomorrow)
_____
_____

3 You are a waiter. A regular customer is making a complaint. (tell / manager)
_____
_____

4 You're going to do a presentation but you're not ready. Your boss is worried. (be ready / in time)
_____
_____

Pronunciation

6 Mark the stress on the words in italics.

0 We think that prices could *increase* next year.
1 There was a big fall in our *exports* last year.
2 Can we *import* this raw material from China?
3 I think we should find a different *transport* company.
4 Are you going to *present* the results at the AGM?
5 There was a *decrease* in the number of complaints last month.
6 Could you keep a *record* of this, please?
7 We can't *permit* this situation to continue.

On the phone

7 Put the receptionist's sentences (A–F) in the correct gaps to complete the conversation.

Receptionist _____
_____

Caller Could I speak to Simone, please?

Receptionist _____
_____

Caller Oh, dear.

Receptionist _____
_____

Caller Yes, could you ask her to call me back?

Receptionist _____
_____

Caller It's Mark Bashir of Hi-Flyers.

Receptionist _____
_____

Caller Yes, she does.

Receptionist _____
_____

Caller That's great. Thanks very much.

A Does she have your number?
B Good morning, Westco Transport.
C I'll ask her to call you when she gets back.
D I'm afraid she's not in her office at the moment.
E Who's calling, please?
F Would you like to leave a message?

8 Complete the telephone message form with the information from the telephone call in exercise 7.

WESTCO TRANSPORT

Telephone Message

Message for: _____

Name of caller: _____

Company: _____

Tel./Email: _____

Message: _____
_____

4.3 Speaking Test: Part One

In Part One of the Speaking Test the examiner asks each candidate questions about personal details, home, work, hobbies etc.

1 **Practise ways of answering these questions. Record yourself then listen the next day.**
Are your answers clear and natural-sounding?

How do you spell your first name / surname?

_____

Where are you from?

_____

Do you work or study?

_____

What do you do?

_____

Do you like your job / work / course?

_____

_____

What do you do in your spare time?

_____

Do you have any hobbies?

_____

Do you think it's better to live in a small town or a big city?

_____

_____

Do you think it's better to work in a small company or a big company?

_____

_____

3 **Decide which of these expressions are useful for**

A agreeing or disagreeing

B giving opinions and preferences

C asking for clarification.

1 I'm sorry. Could you repeat that? _____

2 Did you say …? _____

3 I think it's … _____

4 I agree with you. _____

5 I prefer … _____

6 I like … more than … _____

7 Could you say that again? _____

8 I don't agree with you about that. _____

9 Yes, I think you're right. _____

2 **Correct the typical mistakes in these answers to some of the questions in exercise 1.**

1 I from Bilbao. _____

2 I'm marketing assistant. _____

3 I'm doing a career in economics. _____

4 I working for a small family business. _____

5 My company's name it's Gratton. _____

6 I'm agree with you, a small town is better. _____

7 I not like working in a large company. _____

8 I like very much working there. _____

5.1 Career choices

1 Read the newspaper article about a Scottish company and decide whether sentences 1–5 are 'Right' or 'Wrong'. If there is not enough information to answer 'Right' or 'Wrong', choose 'Doesn't say'.

1 Staff have taken over the Loch Fyne Oysters company.

   A Right　　B Wrong　　C Doesn't say

2 The original owners were against the sale.

   A Right　　B Wrong　　C Doesn't say

3 The Baxi Trust employs over 100 people.

   A Right　　B Wrong　　C Doesn't say

4 Loch Fyne Oysters has made a loss this year.

   A Right　　B Wrong　　C Doesn't say

5 Local businesses have benefited from the success of the oyster company.

   A Right　　B Wrong　　C Doesn't say

2 Look at the underlined words in the text and find words that mean:

1 people who have shares in a company _____

2 people who start a company _____

3 people who live and work in an area _____

4 people who produce food _____

5 people who speak to the media _____

6 people who possess goods or companies _____

Employee takeover of Loch Fyne Oysters saves 100 jobs

Employees of the Scottish company Loch Fyne Oysters have bought the company from its <u>founders</u>. The change in ownership means that everything can stay the same for the employees and the <u>local community</u>.

The company, which supplies one million oysters a year to customers in 22 countries, was for sale following the death of the majority <u>shareholder</u>. Four companies wanted to buy Loch Fyne Oysters, but co-founder Andy Lane wanted the staff to benefit from the sale. He said: 'This is just the result we wanted … and this is undoubtedly the best thing for the company.' 51 employees have worked there for more than three years, and they have been able to buy shares in the company after borrowing money from the Baxi Trust. The Baxi Trust specialises in this type of loan. A <u>spokesman</u> said: 'There have been many studies showing that employee-owned companies are more productive.'

Since its creation in 1978, Loch Fyne Oysters has grown in size and reputation. Annual sales have risen to £8 million and the company has made a profit of around £600,000 this year. The company has supplied oysters to Moscow's Bolshoi ballet, Raffles Hotel in Singapore and the Royal Opera House in London. The new <u>owners</u> plan to continue the 'slow and steady' growth.

The company has also developed close links with local <u>farmers</u> and small businesses. The employee takeover has therefore ensured that the local community can continue to earn money from the oyster trade.

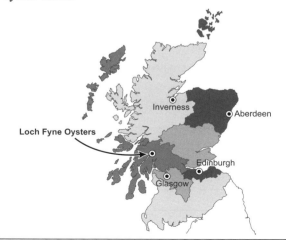

Money expressions

3 Decide which verb does <u>not</u> collocate with *money*. Write the other verbs in the diagram.

| ~~make~~ borrow grow earn save lose |
| spend lend win |

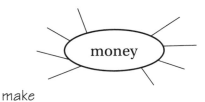

make

4 Complete the sentences using six of the verbs in exercise 3 in the correct form.

1 Loch Fyne employees _____ money to buy shares in the company.

2 I _____ a lot of money when the stock market crashed.

3 The company _____ a large amount of money on public relations after the scandal.

4 If you buy in bulk, you can _____ money.

5 How much interest are you paying on the money the bank _____ you?

6 I'd like to _____ lots of money in the lottery!

The present perfect

5 Read the administrator's 'to do' list and write six sentences about what she has and hasn't done.

To do

phone the suppliers ✓
send them the new contract
book a flight to Glasgow ✓
write up the minutes from yesterday's meeting ✓
speak to the office manager about the security door
give the IT manual back to Sara
buy a birthday card for the MD

0 She has phoned the suppliers.

1 _____

2 _____

3 _____

4 _____

5 _____

6 _____

6 Match the questions (1–6) to the answers (A–F) and write the questions in the present perfect form.

1 you / go to Venice?

2 Alistair / go to Venice?

3 we / use this supplier before?

4 the new boss / go to the office today?

5 you / not / finish the accounts yet?

6 you / be here for a long time?

A No, I don't think we have.

B Yes, he was here at 9am. Didn't you see him?

C Yes, I went there last summer. The canals are amazing.

D No, I arrived a couple of minutes ago.

E No, I haven't started them.

F Yes, he left on Monday. He's there all week.

7 Decide which time expression is <u>not</u> possible in each sentence.

1 I've *already / just / yet* spoken to the office manager.

2 The new owners have been here *for an hour / yesterday / since 9am.*

3 We haven't sold any salmon *recently / already / yet.*

4 Have we had any enquiries about the new model *last week / this week / today*?

5 Has the representative called *since last month / ever / yet*?

6 He has *never / ever / just* read the *Financial Times.*

8 Complete the text by writing the verbs in brackets in the correct tense: past simple or present perfect.

Robson Kline (**1**) _____ (take over) as CEO of Murton Bank last June. Since then, he (**2**) _____ (fire) 20% of the staff and he (**3**) _____ (close) seven offices. In addition, he (**4**) _____ (cut) the salaries of all of the directors. Financial experts say they (**5**) _____ (never / see) anything like this before. In an interview with the BBC yesterday, Kline (**6**) _____ (say) that long-term results are his priority. Several banks (**7**) _____ (have) poor results recently, but Murton's share price (**8**) _____ (rise) by 40% last week.

5.2 Achievements and plans

Talking about results

1 Read the introduction to a newspaper article about a billionaire businessman. What is he going to do when he retires?

Sir Cameron Scott has just retired from business life and he has set himself a new target: he is going to give away all of his money. Sir Cameron, a billionaire, has been very successful in business and also in his private life. Now, on his retirement, he has decided to give something back.

2 Match the sentence beginnings 1–4 to the endings A–J.

1 Sir Cameron ___A___

2 His companies _____

3 The share price _____

4 Investors _____

A (invent) 46 successful inventions

B (found) 11 companies

C (expand) into 25 countries

D (employ) more than 50,000 people

E (be) on list of UK's ten richest people for 18 years

F (sell) all shares in his companies now

G (make) a loss / never

H (rise) steadily since 1987

I (make) lots of money

J (increase) turnover by 700%

3 Write full sentences using the answers to exercise 2, putting the verbs in the correct tense.

Sir Cameron invented 46 successful inventions.

He _____

_____

_____

His companies _____

_____

_____

The share price _____

Investors _____

4 Put the sentences in exercise 3 in a suitable order and add linking words to complete the article.

In Sir Cameron's forty-year career, _____

_____

_____

_____

_____

_____

_____

_____

_____

_____

_____

_____

_____

_____

_____

_____

Exam writing skills: proof reading

5 Read the final paragraph of the article and find six errors in spelling, punctuation and grammar.

Sir Camerons other achievements include a knighthood from Queen Elizabeth II and the french Legion d'honneur. He has also sailed around the world tree times and in 1988 he has climbed Mount Everest. He has setted up a number of foundations to help children in need, and now he planes to give most of his fortune to these organisations.

going to

6 Complete the dialogue with the correct form of the verbs in brackets.

A As you know, our sales of chocolate fall every summer, so we've decided that next year we (**1**) _____ (go / do) something about this.

B Sounds good! What ideas have you had?

A We (**2**) _____ (go / add) a completely new product to our range: ice cream.

B That (**3**) _____ (go / mean) a lot of changes, isn't it?

A Well, it (**4**) _____ (not / go / be) that difficult, actually. We (**5**) _____ (go / introduce) ice cream in carefully selected shops.

B And when (**6**) _____ (we / go / start) selling the ice cream?

A We plan to sell it from Easter until the end of September. We (**7**) _____ (go / modify) the shop windows to sell directly to customers on the street.

B OK, I can see the idea. Now, where (**8**) _____ (we / go / get) the ice cream from? Are we planning to buy it in or make it ourselves? Do we have the right expertise?

A I think we do. Let me explain how I think it could work …

Pronunciation

7 Say these figures aloud, stressing the marked syllables. Note that *and* is not stressed when it follows *hundred*.

20%	<u>twen</u>ty per <u>cent</u>
730	<u>sev</u>en hundred and <u>thir</u>ty
600,000	<u>six</u> hundred <u>thous</u>and
8m	<u>eight</u> <u>mill</u>ion
1½	<u>one</u> and a <u>half</u>
5,347	<u>five</u> thousand, <u>three</u> hundred and <u>for</u>ty-<u>sev</u>en
49,500	<u>for</u>ty-nine <u>thous</u>and <u>five</u> hundred
72bn	<u>sev</u>enty-two <u>bill</u>ion

8 Mark the stress on these numbers, then write them as figures. Practise saying the numbers.

twenty-seven per cent _____

three quarters _____

nine hundred and fifty-five _____

fifteen thousand, three hundred and ninety _____

eight hundred thousand _____

thirty-eight million _____

six and a half _____

ninety-nine per cent _____

eight hundred and thirty _____

twelve thousand, three hundred and seventy-seven _____

In Part Four of the Reading Test you answer seven multiple choice items about a text of about 150–200 words. The options for each item are 'Right', 'Wrong' and 'Doesn't say'. It can be difficult to choose between the 'Wrong' and 'Doesn't say' options.

1   **Read the text and underline the information that is relevant to statements 1–7.**

A PLACE IN THE SUN

The number of British people buying second homes abroad has risen dramatically over the last ten years. The majority of these people are retired, or have taken early retirement. A small number of people work in the destination country and there are those who actually commute regularly from the UK. One city analyst, for example, spends Monday to Thursday at work in London, and the weekends in Barcelona, where his family live all the time.

Some people sell their UK property to finance the purchase of a home abroad, but a large number of people keep their UK residence and divide their time between the two places.

Popular destinations include France, Italy and Spain. A new trend has recently appeared, following the fall in the cost of air travel. People are now buying homes in Canada and the Eastern Mediterranean region. The common factor, however, is the climate. Almost everyone who responded to a recent survey agreed that they wanted to live in a warmer and sunnier place.

Every year, a number of people who have moved abroad decide to return to the UK. The reasons vary and include health problems, family and simple homesickness.

1   A lot of the British people who live abroad are retired. _____

2   Most people work in the country where they have a second home. _____

3   The majority of people in the UK want a holiday home. _____

4   To buy a home abroad you need to sell your house in the UK. _____

5   Spain has a large population of British families. _____

6   People can afford to travel to more distant places now. _____

7   Some people go back to the UK because of language problems. _____

2   **Decide which three statements contain information not given in the text.**

3   **Decide which two statements contradict the information in the text.**

4   **Decide which two statements agree with the information in the text.**

5   **Now write 'Right', 'Wrong' or 'Doesn't say' next to each statement.**

6   **Check your answers in the answer key before you do exercise 7.**

Analysis of answers

7   **Match 1–7 with A–G to complete the analysis of the answers.**

1   Statement 1 is 'Right' because _____
2   Statement 2 is 'Wrong' because _____
3   Statement 3 is 'Doesn't say' because _____
4   Statement 4 is 'Wrong' because _____
5   Statement 5 is 'Doesn't say' because _____
6   Statement 6 is 'Right' because _____
7   Statement 7 is 'Doesn't say' because _____

A   there is no information in the text about what people in general in the UK want. The text is about people who have bought homes abroad.

B   the text only mentions health problems, family and homesickness.

C   the text says 'The majority of these people are retired.'

D   the text says 'A new trend has recently appeared, following the fall in the cost of air travel.'

E   the text doesn't give information about the population of Spain.

F   the text says 'A small number of people work in the destination country.'

G   the text says 'a large number of people keep their UK residence' and this contradicts the statement.

6.1 Business travel

Reported speech

1 Sentences 1–6 report what an airline representative said. Match them with her actual words in sentences A–F.

The airline representative said the flight …

1 would take off on time.	A 'The flight can't take off on time today.'
2 had taken off on time that morning.	B 'The flight isn't taking off on time.'
3 hadn't taken off on time.	C 'The flight will take off on time.'
4 wasn't taking off on time.	D 'The flight hasn't taken off on time.'
5 normally took off on time.	E 'The flight usually takes off on time.'
6 couldn't take off on time that day.	F 'The flight took off on time this morning.'

2 Match the speakers 1–6 with their statements A–F, then put the sentences into reported speech.

1 The taxi driver said _____
2 The travel agent said _____
3 The security officer told me _____
4 The check-in clerk said _____
5 The conference organiser told us _____
6 The airline representative told me _____

A 'You can pick up your tickets at the airport.'

B 'Wait for the conference representative at the meeting point.'

C 'It's €25, please – there's a €10 supplement for the suitcases.'

D 'You're too late to check in now. The flight is already boarding.'

E 'Remove your jacket before you come through the security gate.'

F 'There's a technical problem with the plane. They are working on it now.'

3 Read the conversation between a travel agent (TA) and a personal assistant (PA). Then complete the PA's voice mail to his boss, changing the tenses of the underlined verbs.

PA Ms Vine doesn't want to waste time at airports. What's the train service to Valencia like?

TA It's excellent – they've just started a new service. There are frequent trains and they're really comfortable, especially in first class.

PA How long is the journey?

TA It takes about three hours from Barcelona.

PA What about delays? Is it a reliable service?

TA Yes, it is. No trains have arrived late since the new service began.

PA OK, and what about booking tickets?

TA It's very convenient. You can book in advance or you can buy a ticket on the day.

PA It sounds like a good alternative to flying.

TA Oh yes, it's very popular with business travellers.

Voice mail

Ms Vine, this is Tom. I spoke to the travel agent about trains to Valencia and he said the service was excellent. He said …
Do you want me to cancel your air ticket and book you on the train?

Flight problems

4 Complete the information by writing one word in each space. The first letter of each is given.

1 Please fasten your seat belts for t_____ o_____ .

2 Passengers in b_____ class can board now.

3 Please show your b_____ p_____ on request.

4 To call a f_____ a_____ , please press the button above your head.

5 Flights to London: please c_____ i_____ at desks 12–16.

6 You must not leave your l_____ unattended at any time.

5 Read the airport information at a UK airport. Say which information (A–M) is relevant to the travellers 1–5.

Airport information

← **Arrivals**

| Ground floor (all arrivals) | A |

Departures ↗

First floor

European destinations: Desks 1–29	B
Other international destinations: Desks 30–40	C
Domestic flights: Ground floor, Desks 41–45	D

Shops and Food Hall

← 🏪 Coffee shop	E
🍴 Restaurant ↗	F
📖 Newsagent →	G
🚗 Car rentals →	H
💳 Cash machines ↗	I
DUTY FREE Duty-free shopping ↗	J

Transport links

Ground floor

🚗 ← Taxis	K
🚆 ← Train station shuttle	L
🚌 ← Buses	M

---

1 Mr Q is flying to New York and needs to check in.

2 Ms Z is meeting a colleague from Prague.

3 Mrs X wants to get a train to the capital.

4 Mr Y is returning his hire car to Hertz.

5 Ms V has just arrived from Rome and needs UK pounds.

6 Read the letter from an airline administrator to a passenger. Decide if sentences 1–5 are true or false. Correct the false sentences.

Justgo Airlines
Royal Arcade
Norwich
0845 0909 9839

Dear Mr Nielsen,

I am writing in reply to your letter of 5th July, referring to the cancellation of your recent flight with Justgo Airlines. Justgo Airlines ceased operations on 3rd July and the company is not flying to or from any of its destinations.

Flights home were provided, using alternative airlines, for passengers who were already at their holiday destination. However, Justgo Airlines could not provide alternative arrangements for customers who had not used any part of their ticket.

To find out how to receive a refund of the ticket price, please call the telephone number at the top of this letter.

We regret any inconvenience that this situation has caused.

Yours sincerely

G. Campbell

0 Mr Nielsen is the ~~airline administrator~~. *passenger*

1 Mr Nielsen's flight with Justgo Airlines was delayed.

2 Mr Nielsen telephoned to complain to the airline.

3 Justgo went bankrupt after Mr Nielsen made his complaint.

4 Justgo made alternative travel arrangements for Mr Nielsen.

5 Mr Nielsen could get a refund for his ticket.

Booking enquiries

1 Complete the two emails about hotel bookings using the phrases in the box.

> and one more   Could you confirm
> I can also confirm that the   I write to confirm
> If you are going to   Payment details are
> Please quote this number   ~~We have booked~~
> We now need

From   LMarino

To   bookings@Miramar.com

Subject   reservations LMarino

Dear Sir or Madam,

(0) <u>We have booked</u> four rooms for 10th–12th May (three nights). The booking reference is 983UT.

(1) _____ two more single rooms for the same dates, **(2)** _____ double room only for 12th May. **(3)** _____ the availability of these rooms? **(4)** _____ the same as for the original booking.

Regards

Lisa Marino

From   F_Merchant

To   T Borg

Subject   reservation 21 April

Dear Mr Borg,

(5) _____ your reservation of one double room for 21st–22nd April. The booking reference is TJ98. **(6)** _____ on any correspondence and on arrival at the hotel. **(7)** _____ arrive later than 6pm, please let us know. **(8)** _____ hotel coffee shop serves hot food until midnight.

Best wishes

Richard Merchant

Exam writing skills: punctuation and structure

2 Read the email and add the appropriate punctuation.

dear ms marino

I write to confirm the additions to your booking reference 983UT I have reserved two single rooms for 10th–12th may and one double room for 12th may the additional cost is €390 in total please note that you must present the same credit card on arrival at the hotel we look forward to seeing you on 10th may

best regards

florence bruce

Hotel facilities

3 Read the clues and complete the crossword with words related to hotel facilities.

Across

1 A large room suitable for meetings, assemblies etc.

2 A service for cleaning your clothes.

4 A place to go for a swim.

5 This person carries your bags.

6 The name for the small fridge in your room.

7 This is essential if you want to send emails.

Down

1 This person cleans your room.

3 You can order food from here if the restaurant is closed.

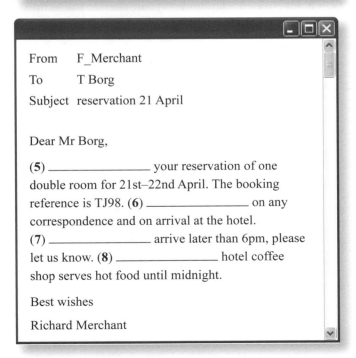

Arranging business travel

4 Complete the conversation between a travel agent (TA) and a customer (C) using the prompts in brackets. Use the correct verb forms, prepositions and articles.

C (**1**) (like / book / seat) _____ to Geneva, please, on 12th November.

TA What time (**2**) (like / fly)? _____?

C As late as possible. (**3**) (there / be) _____ a late British Airways flight, I think.

TA Yes, it's the last flight of the day. (**4**) (leave / 20.05) _____. Business or tourist class?

C Business, if possible.

TA One moment, (**5**) (check / availability) _____ . Yes, there are plenty of seats.

C Good, (**6**) (could / make / me / reservation) _____ , please?

TA Certainly, (**7**) (what / passenger's name) _____ , please?

C James Murray. (**8**) (like / me / spell) _____ it?

TA No, that's OK, Mr Murray. (**9**) (have / account) _____ with us?

C Yes, it's JBA87.

TA OK then, that's booked: one passenger on BA3198 on 12th November, leaving at 20.05. (**10**) (like / me / send you) _____ an email with the details?

C Yes, I would, thanks.

TA That's no problem. Thank you very much, Mr Murray.

C Thank you.

5 You are James Murray, the customer in exercise 5. Write an email to your colleague in Geneva informing him of your arrival time and asking him to meet you at the airport.

Pronunciation

6 Most words with three syllables are stressed on the first syllable, but there are many which are stressed on the second syllable. Write the words in the box in the correct columns in the table.

company   conference   connection   customer
departure   equipment   excellent   Internet
manager   newspaper   technical   telephone

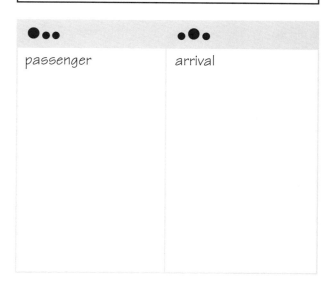

●●●	●●●
passenger	arrival

7 Now practise saying the words in sentences. Record yourself saying each sentence, then listen and check.

1 I read about an excellent hotel in today's newspaper.

2 The departure was delayed because of technical problems.

3 I need an Internet connection to send an email.

4 My company organises a conference here every year.

5 I'd like to speak to the manager about the problem with this equipment.

6 There is a special telephone number for customer service.

1 Read three versions of a memo from a hotel manager and decide which one is in the appropriate style.

A

CARLTON HOTEL

MEMO

To	Maintenance Manager
From	Hotel Manager
Date	13.02

Lee,

People are complaining about the heating again. Didn't you fix it? That's what Arnie said. Can you have another look and let me know what's going on?

Angela

B

Dear Lee,

Several guests on the fourth floor are complaining about the heating system. The duty manager said the problem was fixed, but this is a recurring problem.
Could you investigate and report back to me?

Many thanks,

Angela

C

Dear Mr Henderson,

I have received complaints from hotel guests with reference to the hotel central heating system. I was previously informed by the duty manager that all the necessary repairs were made and that the system was in perfect working order. However, it would appear that this is not the case.
I would appreciate your cooperation in this matter.

Thank you in advance,

A Bosely

Hotel Manager

2 Now do the following writing tasks. Use a neutral style and write 30–40 words

1
- You are organising the annual staff end-of-year party.
- Write a **note** to your colleagues:
  - telling them about the party date and location
  - reminding them that their partners are invited
  - telling them the date by which to confirm their attendance.

2
- You are a hotel manager.
- Your hotel recently hosted its first major conference.
- Write a **memo** to the staff:
  - telling them about the positive feedback from the conference organisers
  - congratulating them on their professionalism
  - thanking them for their hard work.

Products and services

Comparatives and superlatives

1 Look at the table comparing air-conditioning systems. Complete the sentences with the correct system, A, B, C or D.

	System A	System B	System C	System D
Price	***	***	*	**
Small size	*	**	***	***
Quiet operation	*	**	***	**
Rapid temperature change	**	**	***	*
Temperature sensitivity	**	*	***	***
Easy to maintain	**	**	***	*
Easy to install	***	**	**	*
After-sales service	*	**	**	***

*** = excellent   ** = satisfactory   * = poor

1 System D is cheaper than System _____ .

2 System C is as small as System _____ .

3 System B is noisier than System _____ .

4 System A isn't as quick as System _____.

5 System _____ is less sensitive than the other systems.

6 System _____ is the easiest to maintain.

7 System _____ is the most difficult to install.

8 System _____ has the best after-sales service.

2 Write sentences comparing the air-conditioning systems using the prompts below.

0 System A / small

System A is the smallest.

1 System A / noisy

_____

2 System C / quiet

_____

3 System A / easy to install

_____

4 System C / System B / expensive

_____

5 System C / System B / easy to maintain

_____

3 Choose six of the adjectives in the box to complete the sentences comparing travel by train and plane. Use the comparative forms.

> bad   clever   comfortable   convenient   expensive   good   interesting   modern   quick   useful

1 The train ticket was _____ than the plane ticket: it was almost half the price.

2 The journey was _____ , because I checked in only fifteen minutes before the train left.

3 The seats were _____ on the train and I could walk around easily.

4 The views out of the train window were _____ than from the plane.

5 The train had a restaurant car with a _____ range of food than on the plane: I could choose hot or cold food and even vegetarian dishes.

6 On the whole, travelling by train for that distance is _____ than flying.

4 A nuclear power station is planning an open day for the local community. Complete the comments from the meeting with the comparative forms of the adjectives in brackets or *as … as*.

Tours of the site   We should have (**0**) smaller (small) groups than last time.

Free gifts   The cotton bags are (**1**) _____ _____ (good) the plastic ones, but they are not as cheap. The hats weren't (**2**) _____ (popular) the T-shirts last time.

Refreshments   Sandwiches are (**3**) _____ _____ (convenient) hot food. They are quicker to serve and it's (**4**) _____ (easy) to keep food cold than to keep it hot. Soft drinks are (**5**) _____ (appropriate) alcohol for a family event.

Entertainment for children   Acrobats are (**6**) _____ (entertaining) clowns. They appeal to a (**7**) _____ (wide) age range. Inflatable castles are (**8**) _____ _____ (expensive) organised games, but they aren't (**9**) _____ (difficult) to monitor.

5 Read the article from a consumer magazine and answer the questions.

1 How much does a yearly contract with a firm of lawyers normally cost?

2 How many times can you ask for legal help if you have an annual contract?

3 What is the most common problem people ask for help with?

4 How much does a standard lawyer's letter usually cost?

How to choose a lawyer

Most people, fortunately, never need the services of a lawyer. But if you do, how do you choose one? And is it worth taking out an annual contract with one of the big law firms?

The statistics suggest that it's more and more common these days to use the services of a lawyer. There are currently lots of advertisements for annual contracts with lawyers. They are quite similar: for a yearly fee, the firm promises to solve your legal problems.

The idea is simple (1) _____ attractive. You pay €150 a year (in monthly payments) and you (2) _____ consult the firm for legal advice up to ten times a year. All the firms we looked at offer a 24-hour telephone service, and you can consult them by email too. (3) _____ most common reason for consulting a lawyer, according to the statistics, is problems with parking or driving fines. Almost as common (4) _____ this are problems with insurance companies who don't pay out when people make a claim on (5) _____ policy. In other words, these are situations where a simple letter from a lawyer is often the (6) _____ solution to the problem. So how much (7) _____ it cost to get this kind of service without the annual contract? A standard letter can cost about €50, but a lawyer's fees can easily be (8) _____ expensive in a slightly more complicated case.

The conclusion is, if you don't drive, don't claim on your insurance and don't have any complicated relationships with rented houses or employees, it's probably more expensive to take out an annual contract than to hire a lawyer when you need one.

6 Read the text again and choose the correct word (A, B or C) to fill each gap.

1	A and	B also	C too
2	A can't	B can	C could
3	A The	B A	C Ø
4	A as	B than	C that
5	A his	B her	C their
6	A most quick	B quicker	C quickest
7	A does	B do	C did
8	A as	B more	C most

7 Read the email to a firm of lawyers and complete the client consultation record with the correct details.

To: Branner, Bolt and Highbury
From: Simon Westgate
Subject: traffic fine
Date: 11/02/08

I've received a fine for driving while using a mobile phone. However, I don't own a mobile phone and I refuse to pay the fine. Can you advise?

I took out a contract with you just last week. The number is 9934/HT.

Regards

S Westgate

Client consultation record

Name of client: _____

Date of enquiry: _____

Annual contract number: _____

Nature of enquiry: _____

Previous consultations this year: _____

_____

Enquiry followed up by: Richard Branner

Consultation reference: RB/126

7.2 Orders and contracts

Shapes and sizes

1. Rowan is buying equipment for his new office kitchen. Look at the objects above and match them to paragraphs A–E.

2. Complete the conversation using the words in the box. There are four words you don't need.

> best   big   bigger   deep   heavy
> high   long   many   much   round
> small   wide   wider   wood

A

A We need a table and some chairs.

B How (**1**) _____ is the room?

A About 3 metres by 2.5 metres. It's quite small.

B Well, in that case, I think a (**2**) _____ table could be the best solution.

B

B And how (**3**) _____ chairs do you need?

A Oh, I think six is enough. Do you have folding chairs?

B No, not to match the table, but these ones stack up.

A OK, that should be fine.

C

A And we also need a small fridge.

B How (**4**) _____ ? Something like this?

A No, that's more like a cool box. We need something (**5**) _____ than that.

D

B This is the only small fridge we have in stock.

A Can you tell me how (**6**) _____ and how (**7**) _____ it is?

B Yes, it's 60cm by 60cm.

A Oh, that's (**8**) _____ than the space we have.

B That could be a problem for you.

E

B What about microwaves? This one is one of the (**9**) _____ on the market.

A I see. How (**10**) _____ is it?

B Let me see … Just under €500.

A Sorry, I don't think we need anything as expensive as that! We're just going to heat food up, really, not cook.

3. Complete the table with the missing nouns or adjectives.

adjective	noun
long	_____
wide	_____
deep	_____
_____	height
heavy	_____
_____	age

Pronunciation

4. Decide if the pronunciation of the vowel sounds in these two words is the same or different.

height   weight

5. Decide if the pronunciation of the vowel sounds in these pairs of words is the same or different. Write S (same) or D (different) next to each pair.

1 buy   price   _____
2 mail   fair   _____
3 train   plane   _____
4 high   wide   _____
5 slow   now   _____
6 worse   serve   _____
7 cheap   deep   _____
8 work   firm   _____

HOME SECURITY SYSTEMS

	Supahome	Protektor	SureSafe
Price	400	500	475
Installation time	1 morning	1 day	2 days
Level of security	Front door only	Doors & windows	all zones
Easy to use?	PIN code	PIN code	PIN & remote control
Guarantee	5 years	5 years	10 years
After-sales service	6 months free callout	1 year free callout	2 years free callout

6 Read the information about three home security systems and answer the questions using complete sentences.

1 Which system is the cheapest?

The cheapest _____

_____

2 How long does it take to install the systems in your home?

It takes _____

_____

3 Which system gives your home the most protection?

_____

_____

4 How do you switch on and control the systems?

_____

_____

5 Which system gives the best level of guarantee and after-sales service?

_____

_____

6 Which system is the best value for money?

_____

_____

7 Use the information in your answers and the table in exercise 6 to write a short article for a consumer magazine comparing the three home security systems.

_____
_____
_____
_____
_____
_____
_____
_____
_____
_____
_____
_____
_____
_____
_____
_____

Exam writing skills: proof reading

8 Read the text message from a home security company to a client and find six errors in spelling, punctuation and grammar.

We have received your call about a fault on his system! Our tecnician will visit as soon as possibel. Please call 079 878 464 to arange a time?

In Part Two of the Listening Test, you have to fill in the missing information using a word, numbers or letters. To prepare for this, you can revise:

- **the pronunciation of the alphabet**, because whole words are often spelled out in this part of the test and you have to give the correct spelling of the answers.

    Pay attention to similar sounding letters: *T* and *D*; *B* and *P*; *S*, *C* and *Z*.

    Pay attention to the different vowel sounds.

    Remember expressions like 'double E', as in 'S-L-double E-P' (sleep).

- **the pronunciation of numbers**

    Pay attention to easily confused numbers: *thirteen* and *thirty*, *fourteen* and *forty* etc.

    Pay attention to how telephone numbers are given: 0 can be said as *zero*, *oh* or *nought*.

    Pay attention to how dates, large numbers and percentages are said.

1 Practise saying these numbers. Record yourself, then use the recording as a dictation the next day: listen to yourself and write down what you hear. Then compare what you write with the numbers below.

365
15,950
11,560
£27,000
€450,000
three days a
week
PB 10448
00 44 185
663953
34 double 0
7
6th
December
2nd March
1st May

In Part Three of the Listening Test, you have to fill in the missing information using **one** or **two words**. To prepare for this, you can practise taking notes while you listen to English. In the exam, you can try to predict the words you will hear.

2 Look at a sample Part Three question. Predict what kinds of words go in the gaps 1–5 using ideas A–E . Then choose one example F–J for each gap.

A colours	F long coats
B date or place	G TV
C items of clothing	H red and black
D type of media	I wool
E types of material	J next month

- **Look at the notes below.**
- **Some information is missing.**
- **You will hear part of a talk by a retail fashion chain.**
- **For each question 1–5, fill in the missing information.**

Trends for spring
new season's theme: (**1**) _____
main items: (**2**) _____
key fabrics include (**3**) _____
advertising campaign:
celebrity endorsement on (**4**) _____
launch party & press preview (**5**) _____

8.1 Manufacturing processes

The passive

1 Complete the sentences with the correct passive form of the verbs in brackets.

1 These days, mass-produced items _____ (make) on automated production lines.

2 These handmade ornaments _____ (design) by Fabergé over a hundred years ago.

3 We haven't got the goods yet. The delivery _____ (delay) by this week's transport strike.

4 From next month, our electricity _____ (supply) by a different company.

5 The order _____ (send) by road last month.

6 The plant's output _____ (not / increase) any further. It's not possible to produce more bottles than at present.

2 Read about the production of a film for children and rewrite the second sentence in each pair in the passive.

1 An independent studio is producing the film.
The film _____ .

2 A studio in Belgium designed the special effects.
The special effects _____ .

3 Someone films the animation sequences in the UK.
The animation sequences _____ .

4 A technician can record the actors' voices in any location.
The actors' voices _____ .

5 An engineer will add the soundtrack at the end of filming.
The soundtrack _____ .

6 We have completed about 90% of the film now.
About 90% _____ .

7 A company in Spain will produce the copies.
The copies _____ .

8 We are going to release the film on Christmas Eve.
The film _____ .

3 Read about how an insurance claim is processed and choose the correct verb forms, active or passive.

The claims process is quite simple and 99% of the time there are no problems. People usually (**1**) *make / are made* a claim by telephone but details of a claim (**2**) *can take / can be taken* by email or in person, too. It's important that the insurance company (**3**) *informs / is informed* of the accident or incident as soon as possible, even if all of the details (**4**) *can't provide / can't be provided* at that time. After the initial notification (**5**) *receives / is received*, the client fills in a form. This form is the basis of the claim so if it (**6**) *hasn't filled in / hasn't been filled in* correctly, the claim (**7**) *can delay / can be delayed*. The next stage is sending out the insurance assessor to check the claim. After that, all the paperwork (**8**) *sends / is sent* to the main office, where they (**9**) *decide / are decided* to accept the claim or not. With a simple claim, this usually (**10**) *takes / is taken* a couple of weeks. When a claim (**11**) *accepts / is accepted*, the compensation (**12**) *usually pays / is usually paid* by cheque or directly into the client's bank account.

Production philosophies

4 Read the magazine article about a dairy* business. What is the purpose of the article?

*dairy products are milk, cheese, butter, yoghurt etc.

A to give an opinion

B to review a product

C to give information

Back to basics

Ten years ago, Anne Jozami and her husband Claudio ran a large milk production plant. In other words, they kept cows that were milked every day, and the milk was sold to a large commercial dairy. 'The whole place was automated' says Anne. 'The only thing we did ourselves was attach the milking machines to the cows. The dairy company that bought the milk controlled every aspect of the business. All the decisions were taken by the dairy but, on the other hand, it was our responsibility to make sure there were no problems with the milk quality.' Claudio nods his head, 'It was a really efficient operation. Even the amount of food for each cow was calculated by computer. Nothing was wasted at all.'

Things changed for Anne and Claudio when they went on holiday to a small mountain village famous for its cheese. 'The cheese business there was the complete opposite to our operation, and we suddenly saw a new way of doing things: small scale, organic dairy farming producing high quality, specialist cheeses. We knew it could be done, and we were ready to try something new.' The couple's new company is more successful than they imagined possible. 'All of our animals are kept outside and they're fed a natural, vegetarian diet. The milk is processed into cheese here on the farm; it's very labour-intensive and at the same time very satisfying to be in control of the whole process.' The success of the business has been helped by two things. Firstly, Anne and Claudio have been awarded three top prizes for their products. And secondly, the Internet means that they can reach a much wider market than was previously possible. For Claudio, the best thing about their new business is that they combine traditional methods with a modern approach to waste and efficiency. As he says, 'It works!'

5 Choose the best ending (A, B or C) for each sentence (1–5).

1 Ten years ago, Anne and Claudio

A worked in a small dairy.

B owned a commercial dairy.

C sold their produce to a dairy.

2 They were responsible for

A quality control.

B the whole production process.

C buying and selling the cows.

3 The milk production process at their plant

A used traditional methods.

B followed a modern production philosophy.

C produced a lot of waste.

4 Anne and Claudio started a new business

A making specialist cheeses.

B in a mountain village.

C selling organic meat.

5 Their products

A are made by modern methods.

B have been featured on TV.

C are marketed via the Internet.

Supply and demand

6 Complete the sentences by writing one word in each space. The first letter of each is given.

1 People will pay more for individualised, h_____ products.

2 We don't have this model in stock but we can o_____ it for you.

3 The d_____ for recycled glass products is increasing all the time – it's really popular.

4 We s_____ customers all over the UK with our products.

5 There's a lot of new technology in the factory: all the processes are a_____ .

6 With the new machinery, we increased our o_____ by about 25%.

7 We need a special refrigerated w_____ to store our fresh products.

8 We get a d_____ of fresh food every morning from our supplier.

1 Complete the famous quotations using the words in the box.

opportunities problem way succeed

1 'Houston, we have a _____ .'
(NASA Apollo 13 Space Mission)
2 'There are no problems, only _____ .'
(Business proverb)
3 'If at first you don't _____ , try, try, try again.'
(Robert the Bruce of Scotland)
4 'Where there's a will there's a _____ .'
(Proverb)

2 Complete the sentences with *stop/prevent*, *so that* or *to*.

1 Poka-yoke mechanisms _____ problems happening.
2 We advertise on the Internet _____ we can reach a bigger market.
3 A computer analysis is used _____ make the process more efficient.
4 We check everything twice _____ be sure of quality.
5 The alarm system _____ fires developing.
6 The machines are maintained regularly _____ they don't break down.
7 An audible signal _____ people leaving the doors open.
8 Colour coding is used _____ employees know which stock to use.
9 The door has a keypad to _____ unauthorised people entering.
10 We've extended our opening hours _____ reach more customers.

when and if

3 Match 1–8 with A–H to make complete sentences.

1 When we throw away plastic,	A they recycle more of their domestic rubbish.
2 If we burn plastic,	B we create more jobs.
3 When waste paper isn't recycled,	C it increases the pressure on the world's forests.
4 When we recycle glass,	D it produces toxic smoke.
5 When glass is recycled many times,	E it still doesn't lose its quality.
6 When we recycle our waste,	F people use them.
7 If recycling facilities are available,	G it takes hundreds of years to disappear.
8 If people are informed about the problems waste causes,	H we save oil – 140 litres for every ton that is recycled.

Pronunciation

4 Some nouns are made up of two words. The main stress usually falls on the first syllable of the first word: *coffee cup*. Mark the main stresses on these nouns.

1 air conditioning
2 conference phone
3 smoke detector
4 maintenance manager
5 barcode scanner
6 quality control
7 optical cell
8 business school

Collocations with *problem*

5 Match 1–6 with A–F to make complete sentences.

1 Jim's a difficult man to work with. He often *causes*	A *problems* with traffic, especially in the summer.
2 It's our policy to *solve*	B *a problem*, give me a call.
3 What a day! I can't *deal with*	C *a problem* with the supply line again.
4 Everything should work OK, but if you *have*	D *problems* among the staff.
5 We transport by rail and so we *avoid*	E *problems* as quickly as possible.
6 The control system *has detected*	F *any more problems* right now!

6 Read the conversation between Iain, the production manager at a chewing gum factory, and Tina, the factory administrator, and answer the questions.

1 What is the production problem?

_____

2 What is the cause of the problem?

_____

3 What does Iain ask Tina to do?

_____

Tina Hello, Iain. What's the matter? Is there a problem?

Iain Yes, I'm afraid there is. We haven't got any E98 flavouring.

Tina Isn't there any in stock?

Iain No, there isn't. We expected a delivery last week, so there's something wrong.

Tina Someone has made a mistake with the orders, I think.

Iain Probably. Can you contact the purchasing department and get someone to deal with it?

Tina Sure, I'll do it now. Do you have to stop production?

Iain Not for the moment; we can switch to strawberry flavour if we need to.

Tina OK, then. I'll get them to check all the orders.

Iain Thanks. That's great.

Tina Do you need anything else?

Iain No, I don't think so. Thanks.

7 Write the memo from Tina to the purchasing department. Inform them of the situation, ask them to check all orders for flavourings and order more E98 if necessary. Ask to be informed of expected delivery dates.

MEMO

To: Sandra Bofill, Purchasing
From: Tina Rosen, Plant
Date: 19 Oct
Subject: Orders for flavourings

_____
_____
_____
_____
_____
_____
_____
_____
_____
_____

Exam writing skills: accuracy

8 Decide which six words are missing from the memo and write them in the correct places.

To: Marketing Manager
From: General Manager
Date: 28th April
Subject: New product catalogue

The new product brochure discussed at yesterday's meeting with the owners and following suggestions were made:

- reduce the size of the catalogues ten pages
- use full colour
- put the catalogue the website

Could you discuss the first two points our usual printer and look into what's involved with the third? Get quotations and let me know something by the end of the week possible.

Sam

8.3 Speaking Test: Part Two and Part Three

In Part Two of the Speaking Test, you have to talk for one minute on one of two business topics. The questions always start: **What is important when ...?** and there are three ideas to help you speak.

1 Prepare for Part Two by brainstorming ideas on different topics and recording yourself speaking. Write down as many ideas as you can for each of the topics below. Then choose three topics, organise your ideas and speak for one minute.

> **A: WHAT IS IMPORTANT WHEN ...?**
>
> Choosing a business school
> •
> •

> **B: WHAT IS IMPORTANT WHEN ...?**
>
> Booking a hotel for a business trip
> •
> •

> **C: WHAT IS IMPORTANT WHEN ...?**
>
> Choosing a hotel for a company sales conference
> •
> •

> **D: WHAT IS IMPORTANT WHEN ...?**
>
> Inviting a client to dinner
> •
> •

> **E: WHAT IS IMPORTANT WHEN ...?**
>
> Contracting a telephone service provider
> •
> •

> **F: WHAT IS IMPORTANT WHEN ...?**
>
> Deciding which way to transport goods to your shops
> •
> •

> **G: WHAT IS IMPORTANT WHEN ...?**
>
> Choosing a new office building
> •
> •

> **H: WHAT IS IMPORTANT WHEN ...?**
>
> Arranging a staff social event
> •
> •

In Part Three of the Speaking Test, you have to discuss a situation with the other candidate. Your interaction with the other candidate is very important.

2 Decide which of the expressions 1–16 are useful for

A inviting the other person to speak

B agreeing

C disagreeing

D giving your own opinions.

1 What do you think?

2 I think ...

3 So do I.

4 Do you? I don't.

5 I don't think ...

6 Neither do I.

7 What about ...

8 Don't you? I do.

9 Do you agree?

10 I agree with you.

11 I think so.

12 You're right.

13 I see what you mean.

14 I'm not sure.

15 I don't agree with you.

16 I don't think so.

9.1 The future

The future: making predictions

1 Choose the correct option *will* or *won't* to make predictions about how businesses could change in the future.

1 Recycling companies *will / won't* continue to grow.
2 The share price of 'green' companies *will / won't* increase.
3 Supermarkets *will / won't* give plastic bags to their customers.
4 Hybrid engine cars *will / won't* become more popular.
5 More nuclear power stations *will / won't* be built.
6 Manufacturers *will / won't* be allowed to produce as much waste.
7 Farmers *will / won't* grow crops for biofuel instead of food.
8 Aeroplane manufacturers *will / won't* design planes that use less fuel.

2 ZP Electronics are holding a press conference about their new solar-powered games console. Write questions for these answers using *will* and the prompts given.

How / work?
How much / cost?
When / in the shops?
Where / on sale?
Who / appeal to?
Why / not / available before Christmas?

1 _____
   Not until Christmas.
2 _____
   Well, that's a marketing decision.
3 _____
   Less than €300, we think.
4 _____
   All good stores will stock it.
5 _____
   It uses a very efficient solar pack.
6 _____
   Everyone who likes playing video games.

The first conditional

3 Complete the sentences about the ZP games console by writing the verbs in brackets in the correct form.

1 We _____ (sell) more in Asia and Africa if it _____ (be) solar-powered.
2 If we _____ (not use) aluminium, it _____ (be) much cheaper to make.
3 If we _____ (use) recycled plastic, we _____ (reduce) our CO_2 emissions.
4 The costs _____ (be) lower if we _____ (not use) so much packaging.
5 We _____ (have) a bigger impact if we _____ (advertise) on the Internet.
6 It _____ (not be) in the shops for Christmas if we _____ (not increase) production.

4 Match the newspaper headlines (1–4) with the correct stories (A–D). Then complete the sentences using the verbs in brackets.

1 EXTRA MONEY FOR RESPONSIBLE CITIZENS

2 *Oil tanker disaster, warns Greenpeace*

3 **More price increases could leave Parisians on the streets**

4 **MORE WIND TURBINES ACROSS EUROPE**

A If the bad weather _____, the shipment of oil _____ the coastline. (continue / pollute)

B The EU _____ targets for building wind farms if member countries _____ their number. (set / not increase)

C If domestic consumers _____ 'green' fuels, they _____ a tax rebate. (use / get)

D If house prices _____ further, more people _____ homeless. (rise / be)

Strategies for the future

5 Match the words in A with their definitions in B.

A	B
emissions	chemical compounds used to dissolve oil and other substances
fuels	fuels made from renewable resources
carbon-based fuels	gases released when something is burned
biofuel	material which provides energy when it is burned
crops	oil, coal and gas
solvents	plants which are grown on a large scale, usually for food

6 Read the article and choose the correct word (A, B or C) to fill each gap.

Reducing CO_2 emissions in industry: the future

The manufacturing industry consumes massive amounts of resources and energy. Ten tons of resources are used (**1**) _____ produce every ton of new products, and levels of CO_2 emissions from burning coal, oil and gas in the process are also high. Manufacturers are looking (**2**) _____ different ways of reducing CO_2 emissions and reducing costs at the same time.

There (**3**) _____ several fuels which can be burned in industrial processes instead of the carbon-based ones. The use of biofuels – bioethanol and biodiesel – reduces the CO_2 emissions (**4**) _____ a typical factory significantly. Countries like Brazil already have a strong biofuel industry, and now in Europe more crops for biodiesel (sugar cane, cereals, sunflowers etc) (**5**) _____ being grown. Another source of alternative fuels is the waste from (**6**) _____ industrial processes. Chemical solvents are widely used in manufacturing and cannot be re-used, but they can be recycled as alternative fuels. This type of fuel has the advantage of being (**7**) _____ than other fuels for the company that buys it. If we add to this list other waste like vehicle tyres, it is clear that CO_2 emissions can be reduced (**8**) _____ the future.

1 A to	B for	C so that
2 A in	B for	C to
3 A is	B are	C 's
4 A to	B by	C of
5 A are	B is	C will
6 A another	B others	C other
7 A cheap	B cheapest	C cheaper
8 A in	B at	C on

7 Read the comments from a strategy meeting at a factory. Match 1–6 with A–F to make complete sentences.

1 We know the price of coal and oil will
2 We'll have to cut our emissions dramatically
3 Do you think the supply of tyres will
4 If we don't start using alternative fuels, we won't
5 How do we know that biofuels won't
6 If we don't experiment with alternatives,

A reduce our emissions.
B be expensive too?
C rise quickly in the near future.
D if we want to comply with EU regulations.
E our future will be very uncertain.
F be enough for our needs?

8 Complete the newspaper headlines with an appropriate word.

1 **No change in record euro–sterling exchange _____**

2 US and Chinese energy giants announce joint _____ to start new 'green' company

3 **EU smoking ban in the near _____**

4 State-of-the-art _____ installed to monitor travellers at Heathrow airport

5 **Fuel consumption is said to be a key _____ in poor car sales**

6 **GOVERNMENT TO FUND NEW LOW-_____ HOUSING**

9.2 Meetings

will + time clauses

1 Read the extract from a crisis meeting and choose the correct option in each pair.

Artur Thanks for coming, everyone. Now, Klaus, can you give us an update?

Klaus Sure. Well, as I'm sure everyone knows, it hasn't stopped raining for three weeks, and now there is a very real danger that the factory is going to be flooded. The first thing we have to do is try to stop the water from actually getting in.

Amy Can we do that?

Klaus (**1**) *If / Before* we block the main entrances, I think we'll reduce the flooding, yes.

Artur But let's assume that some water will get in.

Klaus OK, so (**2**) *before / until* that happens, we'll lift all the key machinery up onto blocks. (**3**) *As soon as / If* we do that, the damage will be limited. We'll also need to switch off all the electricity (**4**) *if / after* the water starts to come in. Let's also move equipment into the loading area: it's higher than the factory floor. We can leave it there (**5**) *if / until* the water level goes down.

Amy What about informing the staff?

Artur (**6**) *As soon as / Before* we get an up-to-date weather forecast, we'll decide when to make an announcement.

2 Read the extract in exercise 1 again and underline the five action points. Complete Amy's notes from the meeting.

Flood meeting

Action points

1 Block _____

2 _____

 before _____

3 _____

 if _____

4 Move _____

5 Decide _____

_____

Collocations with meeting

3 Choose the correct word to complete each sentence.

1 Have you finalised the *agenda / minutes* for tomorrow's meeting?

2 Why do they always *run / arrange* meetings for Friday afternoon? It's the worst time.

3 OK, that's all for today. The next *departmental / crisis* meeting will be the first week of the month, as usual.

4 Who's going to take the *action points / minutes* for today's meeting?

5 I'm sorry I can't *miss / attend* the meeting tomorrow; I'm out of the office all day.

6 We can't *hold / arrange* the meeting in this room; it's not big enough.

Exam writing skills: proof reading

4 Read the letter of apology and find six errors in spelling, punctuation and grammar.

MOTORBIKE CENTRAL
LEICESTER

28th April

Dear Ms Wilkes,

Please accept my apologise for the problems you have had with your new QX motorbike. I know that your bike was ordered on 2nd March and delivery was expected the last week in March, and it's the end of April now. Unfortunately, the delivery of your bike has had delayed.

The problem isn't really our fault. The delay is due to production problems at the factory. I sent a couple of emails last week to try and find out what the situation is. We have been told that these problems have now been solved and that normal production'll start again next week. Well, I hope so, don't you? We will contact you as soon as we will have a definite delivery date for your bike.

in addition, Motorbike Central would like to offer you a 10% discount on our range of motorbike acessories. I'm really sorry about everything.

Yours sincerely

E. Bridge

Motorbike Central

---

5 Read the letter of apology again and underline the parts that are unnecessary or too informal.

Pronunciation

6 English has both long and short vowel sounds. Sometimes the vowel sound changes the meaning of the word. Decide which word in each pair has a short vowel sound. Practise saying each pair.

1 list — least
2 will — we'll
3 heat — hit
4 bad — bat
5 cart — cat
6 this — these
7 cheap — chip
8 Tim — team
9 sad — sat
10 hat — had

7 Decide whether the underlined vowel sounds are long (L) or short (S). Check your answers in the answer key then practise saying each word.

sh**i**pment	c**o**st	str**o**ng
gr**ee**n	c**au**sed	st**o**rm
n**ee**d	l**aw**s	f**a**ll
k**ey**	l**o**ss	f**au**lty
pred**i**ct	comp**e**te	f**o**rty

8 Read each newspaper headline aloud, paying attention to the words from exercises 6 and 7.

1 **Faulty goods caused business to go bankrupt**

2 **FINANCIAL CRISIS HITS KEY 'BLUE CHIP' COMPANIES**

3 *Experts predict cheap green fuel will compete with oil*

9.3 Reading Test: Part Five and Part Six

Parts Five and Six of the Reading Test both have multiple choice questions. You can follow the same approach. First, try to predict the answer before you read the three options. Then look at the options to see if your prediction is there. If it is, check that the other two options are incorrect. If your prediction is not there, read each of the three options carefully to choose the option you think is correct. Again, check that the other two options are incorrect.

1 In Part Five, you should read the whole question, not just the option. Read the article *European Farming 1*. Look at the options in question 1 and decide which option is correct. Then do question 1 again, reading the whole question. Is your answer different?

2 Do questions 2 and 3.

European Farming 1

Farms across Europe are going out of business, farmland is being sold to developers and country villages are dying. These days, nobody wants to be a farmer. The younger generations of farming families move to the nearest city to study, and they don't come back to work on the farm. The reasons are simple. Farmers work longer hours than in most other professions and they earn a lot less. Farming is not a romantic occupation; it's hard work and, like any business, it has to make a profit to survive.

Most farming businesses are in a difficult financial situation. They take out loans from the banks to pay for expensive machinery, so they have large repayments. On the other hand, their income is not guaranteed. In agriculture, crops depend on the weather. If there is too much rain or too much sun, or if it rains at the wrong time, a farmer can lose a significant proportion of his crop.

1 The article suggests that nobody wants to be a farmer because
   A there are many bankrupt farms in Europe.
   B country villages die when young people go away to study.
   C farming is a lot of work for little money.

2 According to the article, most farms
   A owe money to the bank.
   B make a profit and survive.
   C have a guaranteed income.

3 The article says that
   A the weather is the biggest problem farmers have.
   B the weather affects agricultural crops.
   C farmers can't work if there is too much rain.

3 In Part Six, the questions usually focus on grammar. Read *European Farming 2* and decide which words fit in gaps 4–6. Check your ideas in questions 4–6. Try each option in the gap before you decide on the correct one.

European Farming 2

A large number of farmers with animals run a different type of business. They have contracts (4) _____ big food manufacturers to supply animal products. In this way, they can guarantee an income, but often the price is (5) _____ than the market rate. At the moment, farming in Europe is in crisis, and nobody is sure what (6) _____ if things do not start to change soon.

4	A to	B with	C for
5	A lowest	B lower	C as low
6	A is happening	B happens	C will happen

10.1 Career development

1 Write the words in the box in the correct diagram.

> courses   lecturers   lectures   seminars
> professional development   sessions   speakers
> trainers   training   tutors   workshops

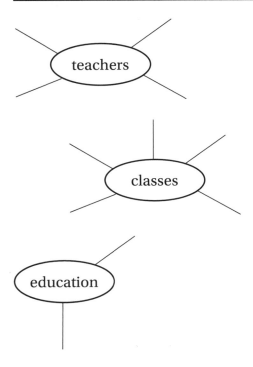

Relative clauses

2 Complete the text using the correct relative pronouns (*who, which* or *where*).

Sudoku is a game (**1**) _____ increases your mental speed and skill. It's recommended for anyone (**2**) _____ wants to increase their brain power, from business people to the elderly. The man (**3**) _____ invented the modern puzzle in 1979 was American, but Japan is the country (**4**) _____ it's most popular. In 2004 a man called Wayne Gould designed a computer program (**5**) _____ generated new puzzles quickly, and in 2005 Sudoku became an international craze (**6**) _____ everyone was talking about. Sudoku software is now very popular; there is a video game (**7**) _____ has sold five million copies around the world. There is also a world sudoku championship (**8**) _____ is held every year. The first competition was in Italy in 2006.

3 Rewrite each pair of sentences as one sentence, using a relative pronoun *who, which, where* or *whose*.

0 I work for a man. He values education.
    I work for a man who values education.

1 I studied at a business school. It has an international reputation.

2 I work with a colleague. She studied at the same school.

3 I did a degree. It helped me in my profession.

4 I had a tutor. Her lectures were inspirational.

5 I work for a company. It has offices all over the world.

6 My office is in a business park. There are lots of facilities.

7 I met a client. His company is very successful.

8 I work in a building. Smoking is not allowed.

4 Decide in which sentences in exercise 3 you can use *that* instead of the relative pronoun you have used.

5 Put brackets around the relative pronouns that can be left out of these sentences.

1 *Don't Just Manage, Lead!* is a course which many managers find useful.

2 Francis Baker is a Creative Director who has worked for leading advertising agencies.

3 The course which I took last year was called *Effective Communicating*.

4 Professional development is something that companies often neglect.

5 I'm going back to the college where I did my first degree.

6 The woman who I spoke to about the course was very helpful.

7 The tutor who interviewed me was quite friendly.

8 The amount of work that you have to do is reasonable.

Describing people

6 Read the texts about three people's experiences of careers development and choose the correct titles from the box.

> An activity weekend   A development day
> A seminar   A university degree
> An online course

A _____

B _____

C _____

7 Match the sentences to the texts. Write A, B or C next to each sentence.

1 This person knew the other participants well.

_____

2 This person can apply what he / she learns at work.

_____

3 This person didn't know what to expect on the course. _____

4 On this course, you learn a lot of theory. _____

5 On this course, you learn about listening to others.

_____

6 On this course, you learn about your role in a team.

_____

8 Underline the expressions for describing people in each text. Write them below.

Text A

great

p_____

good at m_____

good at o_____

u_____

Text B

c_____

d_____

c_____

Text C

good at c_____

great at l_____ and

e_____

A

I'm doing a course in business studies and economics. It's an online course with the Open University. I think it's a good idea for me to do this course now, at this stage in my career. I can study the theory and at the same time see how things work in practice in my job. We do a lot of case studies, which I find very interesting. The teachers are great. They're very patient, which is good, as I ask lots of questions. And they are good at motivating us, which is important because when you study online you can feel isolated at times. Obviously it's important to be good at organising your time and studying regularly. But I don't have much free time this year. Fortunately, my family are very understanding people.

B

I went on a team-building weekend with everyone from my department. It was exhausting! We were in the middle of a forest which was miles from the nearest town. The weekend was spent doing different activities and team challenges. The one which I really hated was when we were taken to an unknown location and we had to get back to the base. I'm not a very competitive person and I don't enjoy being cold, wet and hungry. I was in a group with people who are quite dynamic and confident at work, but they didn't like that activity either – so we made a great team: we came last!

C

I went on a communication skills day at a country hotel. It was all very mysterious; the people who did the same course the previous month weren't allowed to say anything about it. There were people from different departments in the company who I didn't know very well. We did two activities which took all day. In one, we didn't know what the final objective was. Each group just followed the instructions of another group. You discovered that some people aren't very good at communicating, and others are great at listening and explaining. We had a great time and we didn't stop laughing all day.

10.2 Organising a conference

Collocations

1 Match a word from A with one from B to make collocations, then use them to complete sentences 1–6. You may need to use the article *the*.

A	B
book	agency
confirm	budget
development	dates
finalise	fee
registration	forms
speaker's	rooms

1 When we decide the dates, I'll _____ at the hotel.
2 It's organised by a local _____ , which has experience in the area.
3 I've _____ of the conference for late May.
4 Until we _____ , we won't know how much we can spend on catering.
5 We've received completed _____ from all the participants now.
6 How much have we budgeted for the _____? John Cruz looks great, but expensive.

2 Match 1–5 with A–E to make complete sentences.

1 I am writing to invite you	A	a short, after-dinner speech and awarding prizes to our sales teams and sales representatives.
2 I enclose details of	B	attend the conference, which will be held at the Royal Gloucester Hotel in London.
3 Please confirm	C	if you would be available and, if so, your fee for this event.
4 This would involve giving	D	the event and of our past speakers.
5 We would be delighted if you could	E	to be the guest speaker at our annual sales conference in June.

3 Put the sentences in the correct order to make an invitation to a conference speaker.

4 You are organising a training day for your marketing department. You attended an excellent talk on Internet advertising by Marcus Ellacot last year, and you would like him to give his talk to your staff. Write him a letter of invitation:

• saying where you saw him speak
• explaining your training event
• inviting him to speak at the training day
• asking him to confirm his fee and availability.

Write 60–80 words.

> **Citybreak Holidays**
> **Birmingham**
>
> Mr Marcus Ellacot
> Ellacot and Dean
> Glasgow
>
> 11 December

Exam writing skills: completing the task correctly

5 Read your letter from exercise 4. Count the number of words, underline the sections relevant to the task instructions and check that you have divided the letter into paragraphs correctly.

How do you do?

Offers and invitations

7 Complete the offers and invitations using the expressions in the box.

> Can I offer you ...   Good idea.
> Have you been ...   I'm afraid ...   It looks ...
> It's very kind of you to ...   Thanks, but ...
> We're thinking of ...   Would you like to ...
> Would you like to ...

1
A _____ going out for dinner tonight. Are you free?
B _____ Which restaurant did you have in mind?

2
A _____ try this dish?
B _____ very nice. What is it made of?

3
A _____ some more wine?
B _____ I think I'll just have water now.

4
A _____ to any of the typical tourist sites here? What do you recommend?
B _____ I haven't. I haven't had very much free time.

5
A _____ join us for a drink?
B _____ ask, but I think I'll go back to the hotel now.

Pronunciation

8 The plurals of regular nouns are pronounced in one of three ways:

/z/ **as in** *speakers*	/s/ **as in** *workshops*	/ɪz/ **as in** *classes*
_____	_____	_____
_____	_____	_____
_____	_____	_____
_____	_____	_____

Write the following nouns in the correct columns above.

> budgets   businesses   clothes   conferences
> courses   cultures   dates   fees   hosts
> networks   offices   sessions

6 Match an expression in A with an expression in B that means the same. Decide whether the host or visitor would use the expressions. Write H (host) or V (visitor) next to each.

A	B
1 How was your journey?	A Have you been to Oslo before?
2 Is this your first visit to Cardiff?	B There were no problems at all, thanks.
3 That's very kind of you.	C Did you have a good trip?
4 Let's go, then.	D Thank you so much.
5 Everything was fine, thank you.	E Shall we set off?

1 Read the task and the answer below. Decide why this answer received a low mark.

- You are organising a weekend team-building activity course for your staff.
- Write a **letter** to the training centre, Outdoor Business, asking for information.
  - Ask what kind of courses they offer.
  - Ask for a quotation for a group of 25.
  - Find out if there are any restrictions on participants.
  - Find out about available dates.
- Write 60–80 words.

Dear Mr Yardley,

I am organising a weekend team-building course for the staff in my administration department. Could you tell me what kind of courses you offer and give me a quotation for a group of 25 people?

Are there any restrictions on the people who participate in the training courses? I would also like to know what dates are available this spring.

Thank you in advance,
R Brooke

2 Match the sentences below to the four points in the task. Write *course, quote, restrictions* or *dates*.

1 Approximately how much would a weekend course for 25 people cost? _____

2 Are the activity courses suitable for people with disabilities? _____

3 Are there any special requirements in terms of health and fitness? _____

4 Can you quote me a price for this type of course for a group of 25? _____

5 Could you let me know prices for groups of up to 25 people? _____

6 Could you send me details of team-building or similar courses that you offer?

_____

7 Do you have any weekend courses available in May? _____

8 Do you offer team-building courses suitable for young administrative staff? _____

9 I would also like to know about any restrictions on the participants, for example, age.

_____

10 I would like to know if you run courses suitable for a group of young administration workers, on team-building skills. _____

11 Please send me a list of the dates that you have courses available. _____

12 We'd like to arrange the course for May. Could you let me know if there are places available?

_____

3 Write the answer to the task in exercise 1 using the ideas above or your own ideas.

_____

_____

_____

_____

_____

_____

_____

_____

_____

_____

4 Now do the following task under timed conditions.

- You are the manager of Outdoor Business.
- Write a **letter** in reply to the enquiry.
  - Give the information that was requested.
  - Give information about the deposit requirements.
  - Offer a discount on advanced bookings.
  - Give the website address for more information.
- Write 60–80 words.

11.1 Health and safety

Modal verbs: *must* and *(don't) have to*

1 Read each sign and say which sentence is correct.

1

No smoking anywhere on the premises.

A You should smoke in the building.

B You mustn't smoke in the building.

C You have to smoke in the building.

2

In case of fire, do not use this lift. Use the stairs.

A You mustn't use the lift if there is a fire.

B You don't have to use the lift in a fire.

C You shouldn't use the stairs if there is a fire.

3

Only authorised personnel. Wear protective clothing. Shower on leaving the area.

A You should enter this area if you are authorised.

B You have to wear special clothes in this area.

C You mustn't have a shower if you leave this area.

2 Complete the sentences by choosing the correct options.

1 I *must / mustn't* be late for the meeting; the managing director is chairing it.

2 I *had to / didn't have to* take the minutes because the secretary was away.

3 The project is behind schedule so I *have to / don't have to* work late again.

4 The deadline is tomorrow so we *must / don't have to* get everything finished.

5 Oh, you *mustn't / don't have to* park there. It's the CEO's space!

6 You *mustn't / don't have to* believe me, but it's true.

3 Decide which option is not logically correct in each sentence.

1 Contract workers *should / have to / mustn't* sign in and sign out of the plant.

2 You *don't have to / must / should* wash your hands after handling this product.

3 You *should / mustn't / shouldn't* wear jewellery if you operate this machine.

4 We *can't / don't have to / mustn't* eat or drink in this area.

5 Only trained workers *can / should / don't have to* use this machinery.

6 We *have to / can't / should* take regular breaks, so it's not too tiring.

4 Complete the sentences using *should, don't have to, had to, mustn't, can't* or *have to*. Use each modal verb once.

1 I _____ pass an advanced driving test before I started driving trucks.

2 Tomorrow's a holiday; I _____ go to work.

3 I've got too much work. I _____ meet you today. How about tomorrow?

4 If you want my opinion, I don't think you _____ go to work when you are so ill.

5 Will you _____ look for a new job if the factory closes?

6 You _____ leave this machine unattended.

In your break

5 Read the information about a gym and decide whether sentences 1–5 are 'Right' or 'Wrong'. If there is not enough information to answer 'Right' or 'Wrong', choose 'Doesn't say'.

Health and fitness is a growing business these days and we at the Oak Centre are proud to be one of the top gyms in this area.

The traditional image of the gym – men boxing and weight training – has changed completely. Today's gyms respond to what clients have asked for, which means better opening times, a wider range of activities and new complementary services to help people get fit and healthy.

The Oak Centre is open all day, every day from 06.30 to cater for our clients who are business people and come before they go to work or in their lunch break.

We offer typical gym activities as well as yoga, t'ai chi, relaxation and meditation classes. Our ten-minute massage is popular with both shoppers and business people. Our physiotherapists give personalised fitness and nutritional guidance according to your age or job.

We recently opened the Oak Health Bar, which sells delicious healthy snacks and drinks, and our shop can provide you with quality sports clothes and equipment.

Our goal is to promote healthy living and healthy families, and we are looking forward to offering crèche facilities and children's fitness sessions in the near future.

1 The Oak Centre is a traditional gym.
 A Right B Wrong C Doesn't say
2 You can go to the Oak Centre early in the morning.
 A Right B Wrong C Doesn't say
3 You have to pay a membership fee to join the gym.
 A Right B Wrong C Doesn't say
4 The meditation classes are at lunch time.
 A Right B Wrong C Doesn't say
5 You can buy sports equipment at the Oak Centre.
 A Right B Wrong C Doesn't say

go, play and do

6 Write the words in the box in the correct diagram.

aerobics baseball climbing cycling exercises hockey jogging karate Pilates running skiing surfing t'ai chi tennis volleyball

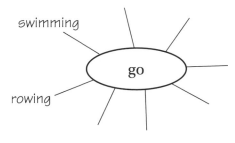

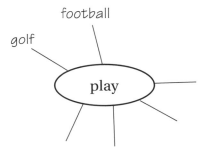

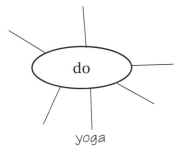

7 Complete the sentences with *go, play* or *do*.

1 _____ is used before games with rules.
2 _____ is used before activities ending in *-ing*.
3 _____ is used before activities with names that are nouns.

11.2 Reporting accidents

The past simple and past continuous

1 Read the conversation between Sheila and Cristina after their annual medical check-up at work and put the phrases A–F in the correct spaces.

A was waiting until after the check-up

B was checking my eyesight and my hearing

C my cigarettes fell out of the pocket

D didn't say anything

E I wasn't telling the truth

F Only one metre sixty ...?

Sheila   Did you get your medical check up this morning?

Cristina Oh yes. The nurse didn't say a word when she **(1)** _____ , then she asked me to get on the scales. I was watching the kilos going up and up but she still **(2)** _____ . Then she measured my height and she said, **(3)** '_____ ' in a sarcastic voice.

Sheila   Really? I bought some croissants for breakfast and I **(4)** _____ to eat them, but when I got on the scales the nurse said, 'only 58 kg!' So I was hungry all morning for nothing.

Cristina Then the doctor told me to take my jacket off, and when I was hanging it up **(5)** _____ , and then, when he asked me if I smoked, I said 'No!'

Sheila   What did he say then?

Cristina Nothing, so I said they were your cigarettes and I was looking after them for you because you were trying to cut down.

Sheila   What!

Cristina Don't worry, he knew **(6)** _____ .

Sheila   Well, of course! I only smoke Rothmans, I can't stand those menthol cigarettes you smoke.

2 Complete the sentences with the verbs in brackets in the correct form.

1 While he _____ the box, he _____ it on his foot. (carry / drop)

2 I _____ through the warehouse when a box _____ on me. (walk / fall)

3 When he _____ the new machine, a part _____ and _____ his arm. (use / break off / cut)

4 Some chemicals _____ in his eye when he _____ to open the bottle. (splash / try)

5 The truck driver _____ a stack of pallets when he _____ into the plant, and they _____ on someone. (knock over / drive / fall)

6 While she _____ the floor, she _____ and _____ her ankle. (wash / slip / hurt)

Pronunciation

3 Many unstressed syllables in English words have the same vowel sound, represented by the symbol /ə/. It sounds like the second syllable in *student*, *teacher*, *problem* and *answer*.

Practise saying these words. Don't stress the underlined vowels.

computer   dangerous   department   equipment
excellent   exercise   fire alarm   information
injury   Internet   machines   responsible

4 We sometimes put modal verbs in the passive in written English, when giving instructions or advice. Read the sentences below, then write the equivalent spoken (active) or written (passive) sentences.

1 Appropriate clothing should be worn.
   '_____,'

2 _____
   'You have to display your parking permit.'

3 _____
   'You shouldn't leave your children alone.'

4 Refunds cannot be given without a receipt.
   '_____,'

5 _____
   'You have to pay the membership fees on time.'

6 _____
   'You have to wear an armband if you're under 12.'

5 Read the introduction to an information leaflet for gym members.

Welcome to the Oak Centre. We hope you enjoy our classes and make full use of our facilities. In the interests of all our clients, we have a few guidelines that we ask all centre users to follow.

_____

Now use the prompts below to write full sentences giving information on the Oak Centre.

1 provide lockers / all clients
   _____

2 place / personal possessions in / lockers
   remember / lock them
   _____

3 outdoor footwear / not use / green zone
   _____

4 all pool users / shower / before enter / pool area
   _____

5 gym: some equipment / book / in advance /
   _____

6 Ask / reception
   _____

7 children / welcome / certain times.
   _____

8 accompany / all zones
   _____

Exam writing skills: proof reading

6 Read the business news item and find six errors in spelling, punctuation and grammar.

caesar Sportswear has acquired the sports chain GetFit, after the announcement that GetFit was faceing bankruptcy. GetFit has 89 retail outlets across the country, and currently it is not knowed if Caesar Sportswear intends to cloze these branches or rebrand them as Caesar stores. A spokeswoman for Caesar Sportswear said, We must to look at the situation in more detail before we can take any decisions.

1 Read the listening script and answer questions 1–3 from Part Four of the Listening Test. Underline the parts of the listening script that are relevant to each question and highlight the key words that give you the correct answer.

PART FOUR

- You will hear a conversation about changes to a company.
- For each question 1–3 mark one letter (**A**, **B** or **C**) for the correct answer.

1 The company is going to
  A take over a competitor.
  B merge with another company.
  C divide into two separate parts.

2 The new arrangement means the company will
  A employ more staff.
  B reduce the workforce.
  C send employees to North America.

3 The company
  A has just trained employees in new skills.
  B has to train staff so that they can expand the business.
  C has no more money to invest in retraining staff.

---

2 Say why the other options are incorrect.

1 _____
  _____
2 _____
  _____
3 _____
  _____

TRANSCRIPT PART FOUR

A It's now official that the company is going to be split into two separate divisions. One division will be based around the publishing activities in Europe and the other division will handle broadcasting, including both television and Internet activities.

B Where will that be controlled from?

A The North American operation will take over that function.

B What does this mean for jobs? Are there going to be a lot of job losses?

A Well, obviously there's going to be a reduction in the number of employees, both here in Europe and in North America.

B Well, that's going to be difficult.

A Yes, it's always hard. But there'll be some people who welcome the opportunity to move on to something new.

B I suppose so – but we've just invested a lot of money in retraining staff in Europe, with the intention of expanding the Internet side of the business …

A Yes, I know. The first thing we have to look at, though, is what this new split means for our department.

B Well, as soon as we get more specific details, we can start to look at the changes and how they will affect us.

A Yes, you're right. We can't do much at the moment.

12.1   The job market

The second conditional

1 **Match the questions (1–6) with the answers (A–F).**

1 Which company would you like to work for?

2 Would you consider working from home?

3 What would you do if you lost your job?

4 Would you change anything about your current job?

5 If your company moved to another location, would you go with them?

6 What advice would you give to someone starting in your job?

A That would depend on the location. I have to consider my family.

B I'd retrain as a lawyer. It's something I've always been interested in.

C No, I don't think I would change anything. I'm very happy in my work.

D I'd tell them to learn to be patient. Things move slowly in this business.

E I'd love to work for Google. That would be a fantastic experience.

F No. I wouldn't like to be on my own all day.

2 **Read four answers to the question *If you had a different job, what would it be?* and put the verbs in the correct forms.**

A

'If I (**1**) _____ (not be) an accountant, I (**2**) _____ (work) in customer services. I (**3**) _____ (enjoy) the variety of work, and I think it (**4**) _____ (be) a job that (**5**) _____ (give) me a lot of job satisfaction.'

B

'If I (**6**) _____ (not work) in public relations, I (**7**) _____ (be) a fundraiser for a charity like UNICEF or Oxfam. I (**8**) _____ (can) use my communication skills, and I (**9**) _____ (enjoy) the challenge of meeting targets.'

C

'If I (**10**) _____ (not be) a travel agent, I (**11**) _____ (do) another travel industry job –

maybe a tour guide or something like that. I (**12**) _____ (not like) to work in a job that didn't help me to see the world.'

D

'If I (**13**) _____ (not have) my own business, I don't know what I (**14**) _____ (do). I like to be independent. I (**15**) _____ (not like) taking orders from other people.'

3 **Match the sentences (1–6) to the prompts (A–F), then write *If*-sentences using the prompts.**

0 It's hard to get a job in that company.
   If I knew someone there, it would be easier.

1 She's happy working here.

_____

_____

2 He's quite lazy at work.

_____

_____

3 He doesn't speak Russian.

_____

_____

4 My company has overseas branches in France and Italy.

_____

_____

5 He works very closely with his boss.

_____

_____

6 My salary isn't very good.

_____

_____

0 know someone there / be easier

A have a branch in Germany / apply for a transfer

B his boss leave / he leave too

C not happy / look for another job

D salary better / not consider leaving

E speak Russian / apply for a job as a tour guide

F work harder / get better results

Getting a job

4 Complete the sentences by writing one word in each space. The first letter of each is given.

1 It's hard to get a job if you leave school with no q_____ .

2 We organise a jobs fair in June, where e_____ and candidates can meet.

3 Would you like to work in a shop? There are always lots of v_____ in retail.

4 Going to a job i_____ can be stressful, but it helps if you prepare well.

5 Don't make any mistakes when you fill in the a_____ form.

6 Many companies contract a r_____ agency to find new staff.

5 Read about this person's ideal job and decide which words could fill gaps 1–8. Then choose the correct options from the list below.

1	A would be	B was	C will be
2	A what	B who	C which
3	A have to	B must	C had to
4	A at	B to	C in
5	A decide	B would decide	C decided
6	A before	B as soon as	C until
7	A lots	B much	C many
8	A no	B some	C any

My ideal job would be a job that paid me lots of money and gave me lots of holidays. My boss (**1**) _____ fantastic: she would appreciate my work and, at the same time, she would be a friendly and positive person. I would work in an organisation that was very efficient, with colleagues (**2**) _____ never complained. In fact, they would have no reason to complain, because our work would be interesting and varied, and our workplace would be comfortable to work in. We would be able to work flexible hours, so if we (**3**) _____ meet our children's teacher or take them (**4**) _____ the dentist, for example, that wouldn't be a problem. If I (**5**) _____ to take some time off to go on an extended holiday to Australia, that wouldn't be a problem either. My job would be kept open for me (**6**) _____ I returned.

The company would be quite large, so I would have (**7**) _____ of opportunities for promotion and for new challenges in my work. There would be opportunities to travel to overseas conferences and to share ideas and experiences with other people in my field, too. The company wouldn't have (**8**) _____ financial problems either, so I would feel that my job was secure.

Finally, I wouldn't have to spend hours every day commuting to work; the office would be a short walk from my home. Perfect!

A covering letter

1 Read the clues and complete the crossword with words related to personal qualities.

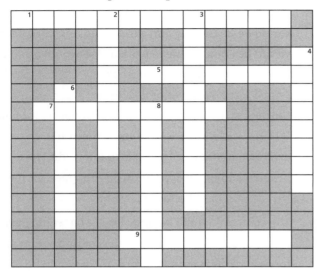

Across

1 We're looking for a s_____-c_____ candidate who is not afraid to take difficult decisions.

5 Thomas is quite rigid and fixed in his ideas. He needs to be more f_____ .

7 Our team is enthusiastic and m_____ about the new project. They are eager to make a start.

9 Simon's never late for a meeting. He's very p_____ .

Down

2 As Art Director, you will need to be very c_____ and have lots of new ideas.

3 We need someone who is i_____ and can work alone, without close supervision.

4 This is a responsible post: we need someone who is r_____ and who we can trust.

6 Robert tends to look for problems, but Sonia has a very p_____ attitude.

8 Rosa is very a_____ ; she aims to be a company director before she is forty.

2 Put the sentences in the correct order to make a covering letter to a prospective employer.

A Dear Ms Brierley,

B I look forward to hearing from you.

C I attach my CV and completed application form. If you require any additional information, please do not hesitate to contact me.

D I also worked for HSBC in my previous summer holidays, when I gained experience in all the bank's main departments.

E I am reliable and responsible and I enjoy working in banking. I am looking for a permanent position from which I can develop my career.

F I am writing to apply for the position of Credit Card Assistant Controller which is currently advertised in the Evening News (reference number PB98).

G I recently completed my degree in economics and I am currently working at HSBC in a temporary post, as a cashier.

H Yours sincerely

Patrick Brown

Exam writing skills: timed writing

3 Time yourself when you do the following task, from the preparation stage to the final check.

Write the reply from Ms Brierley to Patrick Brown and include the following points:

- Thank him for his application.
- Invite him for an interview.
- Give the date, time and place of the interview.
- Give a name and contact number.

Write 60–80 words.

A job interview

4 Read the question prompts and answers from a job interview at a travel company and write the questions in full.

I = Interviewer   C = Candidate

0 I Where / see / job / advertised?

Where did you see the job advertised?

  C I saw it advertised on the Internet.

1 I have / experience / tourism?

_____

  C Yes, I have. I've had several holiday jobs with the City Tourism Authority.

2 I What / be / responsibilities?

_____

  C Well, they varied. One summer I took groups of tourists around the old city, and last year I was based at the information kiosk.

3 C What qualities / need / this job?

_____

  I You need to be interested in people and in communicating, and knowledgeable about the places you're representing, too.

4 I Why / like / work / this company?

_____

  C I'd like to work for a large organisation like this, which has good opportunities for promotion and career development.

5 I What / say / weak points?

_____

  C I can be a bit impatient sometimes, in certain situations.

6 C What kind / training / get?

_____

  I You'd get training in customer care and in dealing with difficult situations.

7 C Where / based?

_____

  I Initially, you'd be in London.

8 C Can / ask / salary and conditions?

_____

  I Yes, the starting salary would be between £18,000 and £21,500, with the statutory holidays and, of course, generous travel discounts.

Pronunciation

Contractions

- In spoken English, it's usual to contract *would* after the pronouns *I*, *you*, *he*, *she*, *we* and *they*. This contraction is not stressed. The stress goes on the main verb.

  I would enjoy that. → *I'd en<u>joy</u> that.*

- When the verb is negative, the contraction and stress is different.

  I would not enjoy that. → *I <u>would</u>n't en<u>joy</u> that.*

5 Read the information in the box. Write these sentences with the contractions, then practise saying them.

1 I would like to apply for this job.

_____

2 She would not like to work there.

_____

3 We would prefer to finish early.

_____

4 I would not consider working from home.

_____

5 They would not increase his salary.

_____

6 He would look for another job.

_____

1 Read the form (C) so that you know what kind of information to look for in texts A and B.

2 Read the letter (A) and the note (B) and underline the possible answers in each.

3 Choose the right answers and write the information in CAPITAL LETTERS in spaces 1–5 in the form (C).

A

DUNLOP ASSOCIATES ARCHITECTURE AND DESIGN
MORDEN PLACE
GLASGOW
078 287 6478

12 May

Dear Diana,

Just a note to let you know we still haven't received the approved plans for the new building. I wonder if you could look into this, as they were sent to you last month.

Regards

David Dunlop

B

Jeff,

Can you arrange for these plans to be sent to the architect's office? It's urgent, so use FedEx. The account number is 564430009.

Thanks

Diana

C

FedEx International Air Waybill

From

Date: 14 May

Account number: **(1)** _____

Sender's name: Jeff Wilson

Phone: 0161 4884 231

Company: Rego Ltd

Address: 28, Sandeman Road, Inverness

To

Recipient's name: **(2)** _____

Phone: **(3)** _____

Company: **(4)** _____

Address: **(5)** _____

Answer key

MODULE 1

1.1
World of work

1
A retail manager
B office manager
C tourism officer

2
0 A (*I'm responsible for the sucess of the shop – meeting our sales targets, basically*)
1 B (*I work a typical working week, Monday to Friday*)
2 C (*I talk to people of different nationalities every day*)
3 C (*I answer people's queries*)
4 B (*I'm usually at my computer most of the day*)
5 A (*I work long days … On a typical day I get here early in the morning*)

3 Text A
0 organise special promotions
1 check deliveries
2 help staff
3 manage staff
4 process salaries
5 supervise day-to-day work

Text B
6 check accounts
7 process accounts
8 supervise staff
9 deal with payments
10 reduce office costs

Text C
11 answer queries
12 give information
13 set up exhibitions
14 lead tours
15 represent the town / country

4
0 work
1 has
2 is
3 deal with
4 is
5 counts
6 don't like
7 don't often have
8 knows
9 are
10 try

5
0 Do you *usually* drive to work?
1 He doesn't *usually* work late.
2 I *never* work at weekends.
3 He visits clients *twice a month*.
4 I am *normally* at my desk by 8am.
5 Do they give press conferences *every week*?
6 She isn't *often* behind schedule.
7 We *often* finish work early *on Fridays*.
8 Our department *sometimes* organises training sessions *at weekends*.
9 He is *occasionally* late for work *on Mondays*.

6
1 check personal emails at work
2 X and Y
3 take too long for lunch
4 X
5 Y

7
In Company X, employees rarely take a day off when they are not sick.
In Company X, staff often use the office stationery for their personal use.
In Company X, people sometimes copy the office software for their personal use.
In Company Y, employees often take a day off when they are not sick.
In Company Y, staff sometimes use the office stationery for their personal use.
In Company Y, people never copy the office software for their personal use.

1.2
Personal and professional details

1

day	*see*	*pen*	*eye*	*go*	*you*	*car*
A	B	F	I	O	Q	R
H	C	L	Y		U	
J	D	M			W	
K	E	N				
	G	S				
	P	X				
	T	Z				
	V					

3

/z/ **as in** *goes*	/s/ **as in** *works*	/iz/ **as in** *finishes*
tries	gets	organises
opens	checks	manages
enjoys	helps	processes
gives	visits	arranges

4
1 Hi Anya, nice to see you again.
2 Hello, I'm Ross McGovern.
3 Excuse me, are you Bart Roland?
4 Hello, Ms Wiseman. How are you?
5 Excuse me, is your name Delemus?
6 Good morning, my name's Maya Lund.

5 1 F 2 C 3 A 4 B 5 E 6 D

6
0 What time do you start work?
1 What do you do?
2 Who do you work for?
3 Do you like your job?
4 Where is your studio?
5 Why is it in Paris?
6 How often do you show your collection?
7 Are you ambitious?
8 Where are you from?
9 Who buys your designs?

7 Model answer:

Raffi is from Birmingham. He's a fashion designer and he works for YSL in Paris. His studio is in Paris, because Paris is the fashion centre of the world. He loves his job and he's very ambitious: he wants to have his own fashion label. He shows his collection twice a year, in spring and in autumn, and lots of celebrities and film stars buy his designs.

8 Hi everyone,
I'm Katherine, but my **friends** call me Kate. My name is **English**, but I'm from Lisbon. I'm **a** lawyer and I work in the head **office** of the Legal Department at PLA. I specialise in insurance contracts. In my spare time, I like marathon **running** and **photography**. You can see my pictures if you click here. I hope you like them!

1.3
Reading Test: Part One

1 1 B

2 Option A says 'mornings only' but the text doesn't specify mornings.
Option C says 'delivers', but the shop accepts deliveries.

3 Text 2
1 C
2 Option A says 'present' identity documents, whereas the text says 'have your photo taken for your conference ID badge'.
Option B says 'leave' but the text gives instructions for arriving because it says 'sign in' and 'welcome pack'.

Text 3
1 A
2 Option B says 'mornings' but the text says '16.30–17.30', which is the afternoon.
Option C says 'at half past six', which is 18.30.

Text 4
1 C
2 Option A says 'open in February' but the text says 'closed'.
Option B says 'closed on the first of February' but the text says 'closed for holidays from 2/2'.

MODULE 2

2.1
Work in progress

1
0 is delivering
1 are extending
2 are looking
3 are improving
4 is holding
5 are using
6 isn't working
7 is visiting
8 is coordinating
9 am giving
10 are doing

2 Suggested answers:
0 On Day 1, he's having a breakfast meeting with the IT manager, Australia.
1 In the morning, he's meeting the department heads until lunchtime.
2 In the afternoon, he's giving a presentation of the project to local staff.
3 On Day 2, he's with the IT manager in the morning and they are visiting the Sydney offices and factories.
4 After that, he's interviewing local staff.
5 On Day 2 in the afternoon, he's discussing the project schedules with the IT manager. / They are discussing the project schedules.
6 On Day 4, he's leaving for Bangkok in the evening.

3 1 D2 2 A1 3 F2 4 E1 5 C3 6 B3

4 **Project manager**
- 0 employ project staff
- 1 set targets for each phase of the project
- 2 hold meetings with management
- 3 complete project on schedule

Team leader
- 4 supervise the work of the team
- 5 give weekly updates to project manager
- 6 meet deadlines agreed with project manager
- 7 hire temporary staff if necessary

5
1 B Wrong (*she says 'I'm having a great time here at Mulligan'*)
2 B Wrong (*'Next week I'm spending three days with the traders in the front office'*)
3 C Doesn't say (*'Are you thinking about applying for a permanent job …?'*)
4 C Doesn't say
5 A Right (*'first, I have to finish my degree!'*)

6
1 option
2 clients
3 great
4 traders
5 short-term
6 degree

2.2
Making arrangements

1 1 E 2 D 3 A 4 C 5 B

2
09.15	nine fif<u>teen</u>
12.30	twelve <u>thir</u>ty
2.20	two <u>twen</u>ty
6.19	six nine<u>teen</u>
1990	nine<u>teen</u> <u>nine</u>ty
1314	thir<u>teen</u> four<u>teen</u>
2015	<u>twen</u>ty fif<u>teen</u>
1680	six<u>teen</u> <u>eigh</u>ty

1 **first** syllable: *twenty*, *thirty* etc
2 **second** syllable: *thir<u>teen</u>, four<u>teen</u>* etc

4
15.30	<u>fif</u>teen <u>thir</u>ty
13.40	thir<u>teen</u> <u>for</u>ty
19.20	nine<u>teen</u> <u>twen</u>ty
18.50	eigh<u>teen</u> <u>fif</u>ty
20.15	<u>twen</u>ty fif<u>teen</u>
Feb 17th	February the seven<u>teenth</u>
Dec 19th	De<u>cem</u>ber the nine<u>teenth</u>
Oct 15th	Oc<u>to</u>ber the fif<u>teenth</u>
Nov 30th	No<u>vem</u>ber the <u>thir</u>tieth
Aug 20th	<u>Au</u>gust the <u>twen</u>tieth

5
1 at
2 on
3 in
4 in
5 at
6 at
7 in
8 on
9 on
10 in

6 and **7**

A
From: Managing Director
To: all_staff@mail
Subject: Phyllis Adcock

As you may know, Phyllis Adcock is leaving the company at the end of the week. I invite you all to join Phyllis, myself and the rest of the management team <u>on Friday lunchtime</u>, for <u>an informal leaving party</u>. Drinks and snacks will be served <u>in the board room</u> <u>from 1pm</u>. Please be prompt.

B
From: Tessa Faulks
To: BWoodcock@Woodcock.org
Subject: Presentation

Many thanks for the invitation to your presentation on Tuesday 12th. I'm afraid I'm visiting our Italian subsidiary next week and so I won't be able to attend.
Good luck with the presentation.

8 **Model answer:**
Dear Tessa,
I'm giving a presentation on 'New Markets' next week and I would like to invite you to attend. It's on Tuesday 12th, in the main meeting room at Head Office.
I hope you can come.
Brenda Woodcock

9 **Model answer:**
Dear Phyllis
I have received an invitation from the MD to your leaving party. I'm afraid I'm visiting the American operation next week, so I won't be able to attend. I'm sorry to miss your party. I wish you all the best for the future.
Regards
Anna

10 I am writing to invite you to our annual seminar on Future Trends in IT. This year the seminar is taking place at the Science Museum, **on 17th July. It starts at 10am**. It is open to all IT professionals, and it is of particular interest to IT systems managers. Please confirm your attendance. Registration closes **on 10th July**.

2.3

Writing Test

1 A Part One (*the text is shorter – 30–40 words, and more informal. It is clearly to someone in the same company*)

   B Part Two (*this text is longer – 60–80 words, and more formal*)

2 3 (*1 does not match because the note does not say where the meeting is, or ask the colleague to call for more information. 2 does not match because the Memo is written to Fiona, not to the department. It does not mention punctuality.*)

3 **Model answers:**

   1 Hi Bill,

   I have a marketing meeting this afternoon, but I'm leaving early to catch the flight to London. Can you take my place at the meeting? It's in room 2.2 at 3pm. Give me a call if you need any information.

   Thanks,

   David

   2 Hello everyone,

   I've arranged a meeting with the IT manager to discuss our ideas for improvements to the internal email system. She will be here on Thursday morning at 09.30. Please don't be late.

   Regards,

   Sue

MODULE 3

3.1

Company biography

1 0 developed
   1 crashed
   2 invented
   3 formed
   4 signed
   5 began
   6 forced
   7 launched
   8 ended
   9 merged
   10 bought

2 1 What did Henry Ford produce?
   2 When was the Wall Street Crash?
   3 What was the aim of the EEC?
   4 Where did colour TV broadcasts begin?
   5 Was 'New Coke' a success?
   6 How long did the dot-com boom last?

3 1 He / Henry Ford produced cars.
   2 It / The Wall Street Crash was in 1929.
   3 The aim of the EEC was to promote free trade in Europe.
   4 They / Colour TV broadcasts began in Europe.
   5 No, it wasn't. / 'New Coke' wasn't a success.
   6 It / The dot-com boom lasted five years.

6 1 B 2 A 3 C 4 B 5 C

7 **Paragraph 1**
   ended
   made
   marketed

   Paragraph 2
   expanded
   acquired
   launched

   Paragraph 3
   persuaded
   developed

3.2

Company performance

1 1 sold
   2 produced
   3 designed
   4 imported
   5 marketed
   6 published

2

/d/ **as in** *planned*	/t/ **as in** *produced*	/id/ **as in** *started*
designed	crashed	distributed
manufactured	developed	expanded
merged	forced	imported
organised	launched	marketed
supplied	published	provided

3 **Possible answer:**

ExxonMobil is a public company. It began operations in 1999 after Exxon and Mobil merged. Its original name was Standard Oil. Its headquarters are in Texas, in the United States. The CEO is Mr Rex W. Tillerson. The company produces fuels, lubricants and petrochemicals and it had a revenue of $377.635 Billion USD in 2006. It has around 100,000 employees.

4 Business is **beginning** to recover from the stock market mini-crash last **Wednesday**. The index **rose** by three points yesterday and there was an increase in activity in all sectors. Experts **say** that the fall in share prices last week was not a real crash, but part of a normal **cycle** and not unusual in **October**.

5 **Paragraph 1**

C, B, A

Paragraph 2

H, E, D, F, G, I

Paragraph 3

J, M, L, K

6 **Paragraph 1**

C founded

B was

A had

Paragraph 2

H grew, became

E was

D rose, dropped

F set

G sold, raised

I had

Paragraph 3

J started

M fell

L dropped

K lost

3.3
Listening Test: Part One

2 A 3

B 1

C 2

D 4

Possible answers:

Words not connected to topics:

A invent, office, safe

B application, fly, time

C computer, paper, share

D material, memo, system

MODULE 4

4.1
International business

1 1 B

2 F

3 C

4 E

5 D

6 A

2 manufacturer → freight forwarder → carrier → wholesaler →
retailer → consumer

3 A (A Scandinavian success story)

4 1 people

2 exports

3 goods

4 companies / firms / brands

5 successful

5

verb	noun – thing	noun – person
compete	competition	competitor
consume	consumption	consumer
export	export(s)	exporter
import	import(s)	importer
produce	product	producer
retail	retail	retailer
sell	sales	seller
ship	shipment	shipper
supply	supplies	supplier
transport	transport	transporter

6 1 Can

2 couldn't

3 can

4 couldn't

5 can, can't

6 could

7 can't

8 could

7 1 should

2 can't

3 Should

4 can

5 Couldn't

6 couldn't

7 should

8 should

8 2, 3, 5

4.2
Business communications

1 1 C

2 D (*introduces the reason for writing*)

3 F (*gives further details*)

4 E (*introduces second point*)

5 B (*suggests possible action*)

6 G

7 A

2 1 J Hallcro

2 invoice 982/08

3 four PC monitors

4 claims procedure

3 **Model answer:**

Dear Sir or Madam,

I am writing about your invoice 982/09 for the transport of our office furniture to new premises on 4th and 5th March. The original quotation for this work was €2,750. However, the invoice you sent us is for €1,500. I think this is a mistake. In addition, the move took two days, not one. Could you please check your records and send me the correct invoice?

Yours sincerely

5 **Suggested answers:**

0 Don't worry, I'll take it.
1 I'll photocopy it now.
2 I'll finish early tomorrow.
3 I'll tell the manager.
4 I'll be ready in time.

6 0 in<u>crease</u>
1 <u>ex</u>ports
2 im<u>port</u>
3 <u>trans</u>port
4 pre<u>sent</u>
5 <u>de</u>crease
6 <u>re</u>cord
7 per<u>mit</u>

7 **Correct order:**

B Good morning, Westco Transport.
D I'm afraid she's not in her office at the moment.
F Would you like to leave a message?
E Who's calling, please?
A Does she have your number?
C I'll ask her to call you when she gets back.

8 **Westco Transport**

Telephone Message

Message for: Simone
Name of caller: Mark Bashir
Company: Hi-Flyers
Tel./Email: –
Message: Please call him back

4.3
Speaking Test: Part One

2 1 I **am** from Bilbao. / I**'m** from Bilbao.
2 I'm **a** marketing assistant.
3 I'm doing a **degree** in economics.
4 I **work** for a small family business.
5 My company's name **is** Gratton.
6 **I** agree with you, a small town is better.
7 I **don't** like working in a large company.
8 I like working there **very much**.

3 1 C 2 C 3 B 4 A 5 B
6 B 7 C 8 A 9 A

MODULE 5

5.1
Career choices

1 1 A Right (*Employees of … Loch Fyne Oysters have bought the company …*)
2 B Wrong (*co-founder Andy Lane wanted the staff to benefit from the sale.*)
3 C Doesn't say
4 B Wrong (*the company has made a profit of around £600,000 this year.*)
5 A Right (*the local community can continue to earn money from the oyster trade.*)

2 1 shareholders
2 founders
3 local community
4 farmers
5 spokespeople (spokesman in text)
6 owners

3 grow

4 1 borrowed   2 lost   3 spent
4 save   5 lent   6 win

5 0 She has phoned the suppliers.
1 She hasn't sent them the new contract.
2 She has booked a flight to Glasgow.
3 She has written up the minutes from yesterday's meeting.
4 She hasn't spoken to the office manager about the security door.
5 She hasn't given the IT manual back to Sara.
6 She hasn't bought a birthday card for the MD.

6 1 C Have you been to Venice?
2 F Has Alistair gone to Venice?
3 A Have we used this supplier before?
4 B Has the new boss been to the office today?
5 E Haven't you finished the accounts yet?
6 D Have you been here for a long time?

7 1 yet (*used with negatives or questions*)
2 yesterday (*finished times, not used with present perfect*)
3 already (*used with positive sentences*)
4 last week (*finished times, not used with present perfect*)
5 ever (*wrong position in sentence*)
6 ever (*used with questions or negatives*)

8 1 took over 2 has fired 3 has closed
4 has cut 5 have never seen 6 said
7 have had 8 rose

5.2
Achievements and plans

1 He's going to give away all of his money.

2 1 A, B, E, F
2 C, D, G, J
3 H
4 I

3 He founded 11 companies.
He has been on the list of the UK's ten richest people for 18 years.
He has sold all the shares in his companies now.
His companies expanded into 25 countries.
They employed more than 50,000 people.
They have never made a loss.
They increased their turnover by 700%.
The share price has risen steadily since 1987.
Investors have made a lot of money.

4 In Sir Cameron's forty-year career, he invented 46 successful inventions and he founded 11 companies. His companies expanded into 25 countries and they employed more than 50,000 people. They have never made a loss. His companies increased their turnover by 700% and the share price has risen steadily since 1987. Investors have made lots of money. Sir Cameron has been on the list of the UK's ten richest people for 18 years, but he has sold all his shares in his companies now.

5 Sir **Cameron's** other achievements include a knighthood from Queen Elizabeth II and the **French** Legion d'honneur. He has also sailed around the world **three** times and in 1988 he **climbed** Mount Everest. He has **set** up a number of foundations to help children in need, and now he **plans** to give most of his fortune to these organisations.

6 1 are going to do
2 are going to add
3 is going to mean
4 isn't going to be
5 are going to introduce
6 are we going to start
7 are going to modify
8 are we going to get

8 <u>twen</u>ty-seven per <u>cent</u> 27%
three <u>quar</u>ters ¾
<u>nine</u> hundred and fifty-<u>five</u> 955

<u>fif</u>teen thousand, <u>three</u> hundred and <u>nine</u>ty 15,390
<u>eight</u> hundred <u>thou</u>sand 800,000
thirty-eight <u>mill</u>ion 38,000,000
<u>six</u> and <u>half</u> 6½
<u>nine</u>ty-<u>nine</u> per <u>cent</u> 99%
<u>eight</u> hundred and <u>thir</u>ty 830
<u>twel</u>ve thousand, <u>three</u> hundred and <u>seven</u>ty-<u>seven</u> 12,377

5.3
Reading Test: Part Four

2 3, 5, 7

3 2, 4

4 1, 6

5 1 Right
2 Wrong
3 Doesn't say
4 Wrong
5 Doesn't say
6 Right
7 Doesn't say

7 1 C 2 F 3 A 4 G 5 E 6 D 7 B

MODULE 6

6.1
Business travel

1 1 C 2 F 3 D 4 B 5 E 6 A

2 1 C 2 A 3 E 4 D 5 B 6 F
1 The taxi driver said it was €25 and there was a €10 supplement for the suitcases.
2 The travel agent said I could pick up my tickets at the airport.
3 The security officer told me to remove my jacket before I came through the security gate.
4 The check-in clerk said I was too late to check in. The flight was already boarding.
5 The conference organiser told me to wait for the conference representative at the meeting point.
6 The airline representative told me there was a technical problem with the plane and they were working on it (at that moment).

3 **Suggested answer:**
Ms Vine, this is Tom. I spoke to the travel agent about trains to Valencia and he said the service was excellent. He said they had just started a new service. He said there were frequent trains and they were really comfortable. He also said it took about three hours from Barcelona and no trains

had arrived late since the new service began. He said you could book in advance or you could buy a ticket on the day and it was very popular with business travellers. Do you want me to cancel your air ticket and book you on the train?

4
1 take off
2 business
3 boarding pass
4 flight attendant
5 check in
6 luggage

5
1 C
2 A
3 L
4 H
5 I

6
0 Mr Nielsen is the **passenger**.
1 Mr Nielsen's flight with Justgo Airlines was **cancelled**.
2 Mr Nielsen **wrote** to complain to the airline.
3 Justgo went bankrupt **before** Mr Nielsen made his complaint.
4 Justgo **didn't make** alternative travel arrangements for Mr Nielsen.
5 True

6.2
Travel arrangements

1
0 We have booked
1 We now need
2 and one more
3 Could you confirm
4 Payment details are
5 I write to confirm
6 Please quote this number
7 If you are going to
8 I can also confirm that the

2

Dear Ms Marino
I write to confirm the additions to your booking, reference 983UT. I have reserved two single rooms for 10th–12th May and one double room for 12th May. The additional cost is €390 in total. Please note that you must present the same credit card on arrival at the hotel.
We look forward to seeing you on 10th May.
Best regards
Florence Bruce

3

Across:
1 CONFERENCE ROOM
2 LAUNDRY
4 POOL
5 PORTER
6 MINIBAR
7 INTERNET CONNECTION

Down:
1 CHAMBERMAID
3 ROOM SERVICE

4
1 I'd like to book a seat
2 would you like to fly?
3 There's / There is
4 It leaves at 20.05.
5 I'll check the availability.
6 could you make me a reservation
7 what's the passenger's name
8 Would you like me to spell
9 Do you have an account
10 Would you like me to send you

5 **Model answer:**
Dear Guy,
Just to let you know that I'm arriving in Geneva on 12 November, at 11pm local time. Could you meet me at the airport?
Looking forward to seeing you.
Many thanks,
James

6

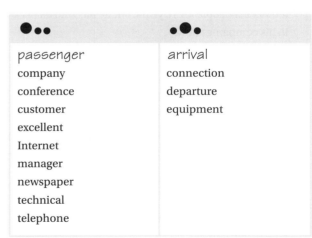

●●●	●●●
passenger	arrival
company	connection
conference	departure
customer	equipment
excellent	
Internet	
manager	
newspaper	
technical	
telephone	

6.3
Writing Test: Part One

1 B (*A is too informal, C is too formal for a memo to another member of staff, B is neutral.*)

2 **Model answers:**

1 Dear all,

This year's annual party is on 29 December at the Grand Hotel. All staff and their partners are invited.

Remember to confirm your attendance to me by email before 10 December, please.

Thanks,

Sandra

2 To: all staff

From: Hotel Manager

I have received a letter from the Franklin Trust thanking us for the excellent service and facilities we provided for the conference last week. Well done, everyone. You did a very professional job.

Thanks again, everyone, for your hard work.

Angela

MODULE 7

7.1
Products and services

1 1 C 2 D 3 C 4 C 5 B 6 C 7 D 8 D

2 0 System A is the smallest.

1 System A is the noisiest.

2 System C is the quietest.

3 System A is the easiest to install.

4 System C is more expensive than System B.

5 System C is easier to maintain than System B.

3 1 less expensive

2 quicker

3 more comfortable

4 more interesting

5 better

6 more convenient

4 0 smaller

1 better than

2 as popular as

3 more convenient than

4 easier

5 more appropriate than

6 more entertaining than

7 wider

8 more expensive than

9 as difficult

5 1 €150 per year

2 ten

3 problems with parking and driving fines

4 €50

6 1 A and   2 B can   3 A The   4 A as
5 C their 6 C quickest 7 A does   8 B more

7 **Client consultation record**

Name of client:	Simon Westgate
Date of enquiry:	11/02/08
Annual contract number:	9934/HT
Nature of enquiry:	driving fine / traffic fine
Previous consultations this year:	no

7.2
Orders and contracts

1 A table (4), chairs (3)

B chairs (3)

C fridge (5), cool box (2)

D fridge (5)

E microwave oven (1)

2 1 big   2 round   3 many   4 small
5 bigger   6 wide / deep 7 deep / wide
8 wider   9 best   10 much

3

adjective	noun
long	length
wide	width
deep	depth
high	height
heavy	weight
old	age

4 different (*the vowel sound in 'height' is* /aɪ/, *as in 'high'. The vowel sound in 'weight' is* /eɪ/, *as in 'wait'.*)

5 1 S (/aɪ/)   2 D (/eɪ/ and /eə/)   3 S (/eɪ/)   4 S (/aɪ/)
5 D (/əʊ/ and /aʊ/)   6 S (/ɜː/)   7 S (/iː/)   8 S (/ɜː/)

6 **Possible answers:**

1 The cheapest system is Supahome.

2 It takes between a morning and two days to install the systems.

3 SureSafe gives the most protection.

4 Supahome and Protektor use a PIN code control system. SureSafe has a PIN code and a remote control.

5 The best level of guarantee and after-sales service is with SureSafe.

6 SureSafe is the best value for money.

7 **Model answer:**

We looked at three different home security systems, Supahome, Protektor and SureSafe. The cheapest system is Supahome, at €400. SureSafe costs €475 and the most expensive system is Protektor, at €500. It takes between a morning and two days to install the systems.

SureSafe gives the most protection; it covers all zones.

Protektor covers the doors and windows but Supahome only covers the front door. Supahome and Protektor use a PIN code control system. SureSafe has a PIN code and a remote control. The best level of guarantee and after-sales service is with SureSafe. The guarantee is for ten years, and there is a free callout service for two years. On the other hand, Supahome and Protektor give a guarantee for five years, and only give six months and one year free callout. In conclusion, SureSafe is the best value for money.

8 We have received your call about a fault on **your** system. Our **technician** will visit as soon as **possible**. Please call 079 878 464 to **arrange** a time.

7.3
Listening Test: Part Two and Part Three

2 1 A H
2 C F
3 E I
4 D G
5 B J

MODULE 8

8.1
Manufacturing processes

1 1 are made
2 were designed
3 has been delayed
4 will be supplied
5 was sent
6 can't be increased

2 1 The film is being produced by an independent studio.
2 The special effects were designed by a studio in Belgium.
3 The animation sequences are filmed in the UK.
4 The actors' voices can be recorded in any location.
5 The soundtrack will be added at the end of filming.
6 About 90% of the film has been completed now.
7 The copies will be produced in Spain.
8 The film is going to be released on Christmas Eve.

3 1 make
2 can be taken
3 is informed
4 can't be provided
5 is received
6 hasn't been filled in
7 can be delayed
8 is sent
9 decide
10 takes

11 is accepted
12 is usually paid

4 C to give information

5 1 C (*The milk was sold to a large commercial dairy.*)
2 A (*it was our responsibility to make sure there were no problems with the milk quality.*)
3 B (*The whole place was automated. …. Nothing was wasted at all.*)
4 A (*organic dairy farming producing high quality, specialist cheeses.*)
5 C (*the Internet means they can reach a much wider market …*)

6 1 handmade   2 order
3 demand   4 supply
5 automated   6 output
7 warehouse   8 delivery

8.2
Problems and solutions

1 1 problem
2 opportunities
3 succeed
4 way

2 1 stop/prevent
2 so that
3 to
4 to
5 stops/prevents
6 so that
7 stops/prevents
8 so that
9 stop/prevent
10 to

3 1 G   2 D   3 C   4 H   5 E   6 B   7 F   8 A

4 1 <u>air</u> conditioning
2 <u>conference</u> phone
3 <u>smoke</u> detector
4 <u>maintenance</u> manager
5 <u>barcode</u> scanner
6 <u>quality</u> control
7 <u>optical</u> cell
8 <u>business</u> school

5 1 D   2 E   3 F   4 B   5 A   6 C

6 1 There is no E98 flavouring.
2 a mistake with the orders
3 contact the purchasing department

7 **Model answer:**

The production manager has informed me that there was no delivery of E98 flavouring last week, and there is no stock. Could you check on this order and all other flavourings orders, please? If there is no E98 on order, please order some urgently.

Could you also inform me of the expected delivery dates for the flavourings?

Many thanks,

Tina

8 The new product brochure **was** discussed at yesterday's meeting with the owners and **the** following suggestions were made:

- reduce the size of the catalogues **by** ten pages
- use full colour
- put the catalogue **on** the website

Could you discuss the first two points **with** our usual printer and look into what's involved with the third? Get quotations and let me know something by the end of the week **if** possible.

Sam

8.3
Speaking Test: Part Two and Part Three

2 A 1, 7, 9

B 3, 6, 10, 12, 13

C 4, 8, 15, 16

D 2, 5, 11, 14

MODULE 9

9.1
The future

1 1 will

2 will

3 won't

4 will

5 will

6 won't

7 will

8 will

2 1 When will it be in the shops?

2 Why won't it be available before Christmas?

3 How much will it cost?

4 Where will it be on sale?

5 How will it work?

6 Who will it appeal to?

3 1 We'll sell more in Asia and Africa if it's solar-powered.

2 If we don't use aluminium, it will be much cheaper to make.

3 If we use recycled plastic, we'll reduce our CO_2 emissions.

4 The costs will be lower if we don't use so much packaging.

5 We'll have a bigger impact if we advertise on the Internet.

6 It won't be in the shops for Christmas if we don't increase production.

4 1 C use / will get

2 A continues / will pollute

3 D rise / will be

4 B will set / do not increase

5 emissions = gases released when something is burned

fuels = material which provides energy when it is burned

carbon-based fuels = oil, coal and gas

biofuel = fuels made from renewable resources

crops = plants which are grown on a large scale, usually for food

solvents = chemical compounds used to dissolve oil and other substances

6 1 A to

2 B for

3 B are

4 C of

5 A are

6 C other

7 C cheaper

8 A in

7 1 C   2 D   3 F   4 A   5 B   6 E

8 1 rate

2 venture

3 future

4 technology

5 factor

6 cost

9.2
Meetings

1 1 If

2 before

3 If

4 if

5 until

6 As soon as

2 1 **Block** the main entrance.

2 Lift the machinery **before** the water gets in.

3 Switch off the electricity **if** the water starts to come in.

4 **Move** equipment into the loading area.

5 **Decide** when to make an announcement to the staff.

3
1 agenda
2 arrange
3 departmental
4 minutes
5 attend
6 hold

4 and **5**

Dear Ms Wilkes,

Please accept my **apologies** for the problems you have had with your new QX motorbike. I know that your bike was ordered on 2nd March and delivery was expected the last week in March, and it's the end of April now. Unfortunately, the delivery of your bike has **been** delayed.

The problem isn't really our fault. The delay is due to production problems at the factory. I sent a couple of emails last week to try and find out what the situation is. We have been told that these problems have now been solved and that normal production **will** start again next week. Well, I hope so, don't you? We will contact you as soon as we **have** a definite delivery date for your bike.

In addition, QX would like to offer you a 10% discount on our range of motorbike **accessories**. I'm really sorry about everything.

Yours sincerely
E. Bridge
Motorbike Central

6 **Short vowels:**
1 list
2 will
3 hit
4 bat
5 cat
6 this
7 chip
8 Tim
9 sat
10 hat

7
shipment	S
green	L
need	L
key	L
predict	S
cost	S
caused	L
laws	L
loss	S
compete	L
strong	S
storm	L
fall	L

faulty	S
forty	L

9.3
Reading Test: Part Five and Part Six

1 C is correct. Statements B and C are both true according to what the text suggests, but they are not reasons why 'nobody wants to be a farmer'.

2 2 A (*They take out loans from the banks … their income is not guaranteed.*) 3 B (*crops depend on the weather.*)

3 4 B with
5 B lower
6 C will happen

MODULE 10

10.1
Career development

1 **teachers**
lecturers
speakers
trainers
tutors
classes
courses
lectures
seminars
sessions
workshops
education
professional development
training

2 1 which
2 who
3 who
4 where
5 which
6 which
7 which
8 which

3 0 I work for a man who values education.
1 I studied at a business school **which** has an international reputation.
2 I work with a colleague **who** studied at the same school.
3 I did a degree **which** helped me in my profession.
4 I had a tutor **whose** lectures were inspirational.
5 I work for a company **which** has offices all over the world.

6 My office is in a business park **where** there are lots of facilities.

7 I met a client **whose** company is very successful.

8 I work in a building **where** smoking is not allowed.

4 Sentences 1, 2, 3 and 5. (*You are less likely to use 'that' in sentence 2, as 'colleague' refers to a person, so 'who' sounds more natural.*)

5 1 *Don't Just Manage, Lead!* is a course (which) many managers find useful.

2 Francis Baker is a Creative Director who has worked for leading advertising agencies.

3 The course (which) I took last year was called *Effective Communicating*.

4 Professional development is something (that) companies often neglect.

5 I'm going back to the college where I did my first degree.

6 The woman (who) I spoke to about the course was very helpful.

7 The tutor who interviewed me was quite friendly.

8 The amount of work (that) you have to do is reasonable.

6 A An online course

B An activity weekend

C A development day

7 1 B (*I was in a group with people who are quite dynamic and confident at work …*)

2 A (*I can … see how things work in practice in my job.*)

3 C (*It was all very mysterious …*)

4 A (*I can study the theory … We do a lot of case studies …*)

5 C (*You discovered that … others are great at listening …*)

6 B (*I went on a team-building weekend … we made a great team …*)

8 **Text A**

great

patient

good at motivating (us)

good at organising (time)

understanding

Text B

competitive

dynamic

confident

Text C

good at communicating

great at listening and explaining

10.2
Organising a conference

1 1 When we decide the dates, I'll **book a room / book rooms** at the hotel.

2 It's organised by a local **development agency**, which has experience in the area.

3 I've **confirmed the dates** of the conference for late May.

4 Until we **finalise the budget**, we won't know how much we can spend on catering.

5 We've received completed **registration forms** from all the participants now.

6 How much have we budgeted for the **speaker's fee**? John Cruz looks great, but expensive.

2 and **3**

1 E   4 A   2 D   5 B   3 C

4 **Model answer:**

Dear Mr Ellacott,

I attended your talk on Internet advertising at the Northern Chamber of Commerce and I thought it was very relevant and interesting.

I am currently organising a development day on the topic of 'Marketing and the Internet' for a group of about forty staff. I would be delighted if you could deliver your talk as part of the event. I enclose details of the event and of our company.

Please confirm your availability and your fee.

Yours sincerely,

6 1 C H   2 A H   3 D V   4 E H   5 B V

7 1

A *We're thinking of* going out for dinner tonight. Are you free?

B *Good idea.* Which restaurant did you have in mind?

2

A *Would you like to* try this dish?

B *It looks* very nice. What is it made of?

3

A *Can I offer you* some more wine?

B *Thanks, but* I think I'll just have water now.

4

A *Have you been* to any of the typical tourist sites here? What do you recommend?

B *I'm afraid* I haven't. I haven't had very much free time.

5

A *Would you like to* join us for a drink?

B *It's very kind of you to* ask, but I think I'll go back to the hotel now.

8

/z/ as in *speakers*	/s/ as in *workshops*	/iz/ as in *classes*
clothes	budgets	businesses
cultures	dates	conferences
fees	hosts	courses
sessions	networks	offices

10.3
Writing Test: Part Two

1 The answer received a low mark because it copied too much from the instructions. You should try to express the same ideas in your own words.

2 Ask what kind of courses they offer: 6, 8, 10
Ask for a quotation for a group of 25: 1, 4, 5
Find out if there are any restrictions on participants: 2, 3, 9
Find out about available dates: 7, 11, 12

3 **Model answer:**
Dear Mr Yardley,
I am organising some training for administrative staff and I see from your website that you run residential weekend courses.
I would like to know if you have courses suitable for a group of young administration workers, on team-building skills.
Could you let me know prices for groups of up to 25 people and also if the activity courses are suitable for people with disabilities?
Please send me a list of the dates that you have courses available.
Thank you in advance,
R Brooke

4 **Model answer:**
Dear Ms Brooke,
Thank you for your enquiry about our courses. We offer a team-building activity weekend which is suitable for people working in most areas of business. Please see the enclosed leaflet which gives full details, and the restrictions on participants. The price will be €2,500–€3,000, with a 10% deposit to be paid at the time of booking. There is a 5% discount on bookings made over two months in advance. Please also see our website OutdoorBusiness.co.uk.
Best regards
Tom Yardley

MODULE 11

11.1
Health and safety

1 1 B   2 A   3 B

2
1 mustn't
2 had to
3 have to
4 must
5 mustn't
6 don't have to

3
1 mustn't
2 don't have to
3 should
4 don't have to
5 don't have to
6 can't

4
1 had to
2 don't have to
3 can't
4 should
5 have to
6 mustn't

5
1 B Wrong (*The traditional image of the gym has changed completely.*)
2 A Right (*open all day, every day from 6.30 …*)
3 C Doesn't say
4 C Doesn't say
5 A Right (*our shop can provide you with quality sports clothes and equipment.*)

6

go	play	do
swimming	football	yoga
rowing	golf	aerobics
climbing	baseball	exercises
cycling	hockey	karate
jogging	tennis	Pilates
running	volleyball	t'ai chi
skiing		
surfing		

7
1 **play** is used before games with rules.
2 **go** is used before activities ending in -*ing*.
3 **do** is used before activities with names that are nouns.

11.2
Reporting accidents

1 1 B   2 D   3 F   4 A   5 C   6 E

2
1 was carrying / dropped
2 was walking / fell
3 was using / broke off / cut
4 splashed / was trying
5 knocked over / was driving / fell
6 was washing / slipped / hurt

4
1 'You have to / should / must wear appropriate clothing.'
2 Parking permits must be displayed.
3 Children must not be left unattended.
4 'We can't give refunds if you don't have the receipt.'
5 Membership fees must be paid on time.
6 Armbands must be worn by all children under 12.

5 **Model answer:**
1 We provide lockers for all clients.
2 Please place all your personal possessions in the lockers and remember to lock them.
3 Outdoor footwear should not be used in the green zone.
4 All pool users should shower before entering the pool area.
5 In the gym, some equipment must be booked in advance.
6 Ask at reception.
7 Children are welcome at certain times.
8 They must be accompanied in all zones.

6 **Caesar** Sportswear has acquired the sports chain GetFit, after the announcement that GetFit was **facing** bankruptcy. GetFit has 89 retail outlets across the country, and currently it is not **known** if Caesar Sportswear intends to **close** these branches or rebrand them as Caesar stores. A spokeswoman for Caesar Sportswear said, **'We must look** at the situation in more detail before we can take any decisions.**'**

11.3
Listening Test: Part Four

I 1 C 2 B 3 A

Question 1:
A: It's now official that the company is going to be split into two separate divisions.

Question 2:
A: Well, obviously there's going to be a reduction in the number of employees, both here in Europe and in North America.

Question 3:
B: I suppose so – but we've just invested a lot of money in retraining staff in Europe, with the intention of expanding the Internet side of the business …

2 In 1, option A is incorrect because neither *take over* nor *competitor* are mentioned in the text. Option B is incorrect because *merge* is not mentioned. In addition, options A and B both refer to other companies, but no other companies are mentioned in the text.

In 2, option A is incorrect because *reduction* means the opposite of *employ more*. Option C is incorrect because the

text says the company will reduce the number of employees in North America, not send people there.

In 3, option B is incorrect because they don't have to train staff; they *have just trained* staff. Option C is incorrect because the text says they have invested in training but doesn't mention money specifically.

MODULE 12

12.1
The job market

I 1 E   2 F   3 B   4 C   5 A   6 D

2
1 was not / wasn't
2 would work / 'd work
3 would enjoy / 'd enjoy
4 would be
5 would give
6 did not work / didn't work
7 would be / 'd be
8 could / would be able to
9 would enjoy / 'd enjoy
10 was not / wasn't / weren't
11 would do / 'd do
12 would not like / wouldn't like
13 did not have / didn't have
14 would do / 'd do
15 would not like / wouldn't like / don't like

3
0 0 If I knew someone there, it would be easier.
1 C If she wasn't happy here, she would look for another job.
2 F If he worked harder, he would get better results.
3 E If he spoke Russian, he would apply for a job as a tour guide.
4 A If it had a branch in Germany, I would apply for a transfer.
5 B If his boss left, he would leave too.
6 D If the salary was better, I wouldn't consider leaving.

4
1 qualifications
2 employers
3 vacancies
4 interview
5 application
6 recruitment

5
1 A would be
2 B who
3 C had to
4 B to
5 C decided

6 C until
7 A lots
8 C any

12.2
Job applications

1

¹s	e	l	f	²c	o	n	f	³i	d	e	n	t	
				r				n					
				e				d					⁴r
				a		⁵f	l	e	x	i	b	l	e
		⁶p		t				p					l
	⁷m	o	t	i	v	⁸a	t	e	d				i
		s		v		m		n					a
		i		e		b		d					b
		t				i		e					l
		i				t		n					e
		v				i		t					
		e				o							
					⁹p	u	n	c	t	u	a	l	
						s							

2 1 A 2 F 3 G 4 D 5 E 6 C 7 B 8 H

3 **Model answer**:

Dear Mr Brown,

Thank you for your application for the post of Credit Card Assistant Controller at Winthrop Bank.

I would like to invite you to attend an interview for this position. The interview will take place at Winthrop Bank's head office at Winthrop House in York, at 09.45 on 2nd September. Please confirm your attendance by telephoning Susan on extension 1356 on the number at the head of this letter.

I look forward to meeting you.

Yours sincerely,

F. Brierley

4 0 Where did you see the job advertised?
1 Do you have any experience in tourism?
2 What were your responsibilities?
3 What qualities do you need in this job?
4 Why would you like to work for this company?
5 What would you say your weak points were?
6 What kind of training would I get?
7 Where would I be based?
8 Can I ask you about salary and conditions?

5 1 I'd <u>like</u> to apply for this job.
2 She <u>would</u>n't <u>like</u> to work there.
3 We'd pre<u>fer</u> to finish early.
4 I <u>would</u>n't con<u>sider</u> working from home.
5 They <u>would</u>n't in<u>crease</u> his salary.
6 He'd <u>look</u> for another job.

12.3
Reading Test: Part Seven

3 1 564430009
2 DAVID DUNLOP
3 078 287 6478
4 DUNLOP ASSOCIATES ARCHITECTURE AND DESIGN
5 MORDEN PLACE, GLASGOW